100+ IDEAS TO INSPIRE
SMART SPACES AND CREATIVE PLACES

ELISABETH DOUCETT is executive director of the Curtis Memorial Library in Brunswick, Maine, and the author of *New Routes to Library Success, What They Don't Teach You in Library School*, and *Creating Your Library Brand*. She holds a BA from Smith College, an MLS from Simmons College, and an MBA in marketing from the J. L. Kellogg School of Management at Northwestern University.

ISBNs
978-0-8389-4718-0 (paper)
978-0-8389-4730-2 (PDF)
978-0-8389-4731-9 (ePub)
978-0-8389-4732-6 (Kindle)

Library of Congress Cataloging-in-Publication Data
Names: Doucett, Elisabeth, author.
Title: 100+ ideas to inspire smart spaces and creative places / Elisabeth Doucett.
Other titles: One hundred plus ideas to inspire smart spaces and creative places
Description: Chicago : ALA Editions, 2020. | Series: Instant impact for your library | Includes bibliographical references. | Summary: "This book provides over 100 space and design ideas that libraries can model"—Provided by publisher.
Identifiers: LCCN 2019051444 (print) | LCCN 2019051445 (ebook) | ISBN 9780838947180 (paperback) | ISBN 9780838947302 (pdf) | ISBN 9780838947319 (epub) | ISBN 9780838947326 (kindle edition)
Subjects: LCSH: Libraries—Space utilization. | Library buildings—United States—Case studies.
Classification: LCC Z679.55 .D68 2020 (print) | LCC Z679.55 (ebook) | DDC 022/.3—dc23
LC record available at https://lccn.loc.gov/2019051444
LC ebook record available at https://lccn.loc.gov/2019051445

Book design by Alejandra Diaz in the FreightText Pro, Protipo and Rift Soft typefaces.

♾ This paper meets the requirements of ANSI/NISO Z39.48-1992 (Permanence of Paper).

Printed in the United States of America
24 23 22 21 20   5 4 3 2 1

CONTENTS

ACKNOWLEDGMENTS

I would like to thank my brother, Jamie Doucett, who took many of the photographs in this book. He has always been a wonderful photographer, and it was a real treat to have him take photographs of Curtis Memorial Library.

And, speaking of Curtis, I work with a group of wonderful people there. The librarians and staff are smart, funny, extraordinarily creative, and willing to try almost anything to ensure our library is the best it can be for our community. Most of the examples shared in this book of Curtis spaces happened because of their ingenuity and willingness to explore.

Curtis also has a large and very dedicated cadre of volunteers who raise money to support the library and who do an infinite number of jobs within it. This gives the staff the free time and resources to produce their magic.

And, finally, the board of directors at Curtis has always been supportive and smart about how they oversee the library. They have trusted the library staff to do their absolute best, and I don't think they have ever been disappointed.

Thank you to all of these people for their dedication to such an amazing community institution as Curtis Memorial Library.

INTRODUCTION

We all know that life is getting busier. As librarians we strive every day to listen to our community, provide the services that enrich the lives of our users, and occasionally find the time to do some reading that furthers our professional skills and sparks our creativity.

I wrote this book for those small chunks of time when librarians have the energy and interest to learn something new that might be useful at their library. The chapters are short and meant to stand alone, so you can read whatever captures your interest. I provided examples of space and design elements that can be used by libraries. There are photographs, so you can see how some of these space ideas look in real life. At the end of each chapter, I have provided a few online resources that I found useful and that should assist you in learning more about a specific topic.

I try to keep my eyes open, and when I see a good idea, no matter where I find it, I think about how I might be able to use that idea at my library. At the end of the day, my goal is just like that of every librarian. I want to make sure my library is doing useful, relevant work and that it is an institution valued and frequently visited by its community. I hope this book will help you in that endeavor.

WHY THESE IDEAS MATTER

When I started writing this book, I wanted to identify space and design ideas that libraries could model or that would spur the development of new ideas in readers' minds. Here are the key reasons why all of these ideas can make a difference in your library:

- People today want experiences. They want to be entertained and educated. Libraries are not exempt from this expectation. If you can ensure that a visit to the library will include the opportunity to experience something new (art/displays/hands-on exhibits/etc.), it will greatly enhance the likelihood that your patrons will visit the library on a regular basis.

Plus, given that libraries have plenty of space for their books, space is an obvious tool with which libraries can work.

- Many of these ideas will draw people into your library who don't visit often or, in some cases, ever. The ideas are meant to be fun, different, and of a nature that will appeal to lots of people, not just those who visit the library regularly. Innovative ideas will help expand the number of people who experience your space. Plus, once you've got those folks in the door, you'll have the chance to share all of the other wonderful things your library can do for them.

- Some of the ideas included in this book are good for library staff and visitors just because they improve the health or attractiveness of the library space. For example, green spaces are innately eye-catching. They encourage stopping, relaxing, and enjoying, all of which are beneficial to our health. They also add to the oxygen level of the space they inhabit, and more oxygen is good for everyone!

- Libraries are still accused by critics of being dusty, musty, old spaces. I think nothing can do a better job of combating that image than new ideas, demonstrated in a very physical, real, and unexpected way. Imagine if people came to town in the summer and were told at the visitor's center, "Don't miss visiting the bathrooms at the library!" (Keep reading if you want to know what that means.)

- Creating spaces for specific groups, such as millennials, is a fairly simple way of beginning to build a relationship with that group. You probably don't want to turn your whole library into a millennial-enticing zone, but it can't hurt (and might help) to think about what they want and how you might provide them with that. At the same time an idea that is meant for millennials must just as easily appeal to others. You never know until you try.

- Space has the potential to amplify the standards espoused by a library. If a space can articulate what your library values and believes in, it can act as a powerful tool to reinforce that message to your community. Instead of walking into a library and feeling as if your surroundings resemble those of other libraries you've visited, imagine how powerful it would be to walk into your local library and immediately experience what is important to that organization and what makes it unique and relevant to its community.

- Libraries were built to last, and they weren't meant to change much in terms of their physical presence. In the 1960s and '70s, you could probably walk into almost any average library in America and understand very quickly where the books were kept, how you were supposed to go through the process of borrowing books, and where you were meant to go if you had questions. Libraries were *the* source of information and of books to borrow, and no one expected much more from them than a predictable experience and available reading materials.

  Obviously, things have changed. The internet is a constantly shifting kaleidoscope of ideas, information, and entertainment, and that has become the new norm. By creating a library with spaces that reflect that vibrancy and fluidity, we will be taking yet another step to define today's library as relevant, exciting, and an institution worth supporting.

- Most of the ideas in this book will help you move your library from being transactional (someone gets a book, checks out that book, and leaves the library) to being much more experiential (a patron sits down in a comfortable chair in the sun to spend some time reading a book, and in the process ends up chatting with a newcomer to the community or watching a program). Experiential use of the library develops much stronger ties between the library user and the institution and helps create a sense of community and belonging. That's worth a great deal to both the library and the people who use it.

Pick a chapter that looks interesting and jump in. You don't need to read the chapters in any particular order, nor do you need to read all of the chapters in the book. Keep in mind that some of these ideas can be combined. For example, you might create Instagram bait by developing a green space in your library or by turning your bathroom into an art display. If that sounds confusing or weird, keep reading!

BIOPHILIC DESIGN
INVITING MOTHER NATURE INTO YOUR LIBRARY

Biophilic design is the inclusion of green, living things into a space with the goal of making that environment healthier, more enjoyable, and more attractive. It advocates the use of natural light, natural materials, living greenery, water, and the sounds and smells of nature.

The term was coined by Edward O. Wilson, who in 1984 published a short book on the topic, titled *Biophilia*. He identified biophilia as "humans' innate tendency to focus on living things, as opposed to the inanimate."

People like seeing green inside a building just because it looks nice and creates a pleasant environment. However, biophilic design goes beyond simply creating an attractive space. It is also championed as a method to lower stress, improve the quality of oxygen, and increase creativity and innovation. Adding greenery to a space also helps make that space a quieter and more contemplative environment.

How do you know biophilic design when you see it? Think about what you might see on a walk outside. Water flowing across rocks in a stream, moss on the banks of a river, lawns, flowerbeds, and rows of trees all would qualify.

When you see those elements inside a building or in an urban environment, you are seeing biophilic design. Biophilia has become very popular as a design concept, and you are likely to see some version of it in almost every type of public space, including hospitals, malls, retail centers, office buildings, schools, hotels, and homes.

The Ford Foundation atrium on 42nd Street in New York City is a wonderful example of biophilic design at its best. When you walk into the lobby from the busy, urban street, you feel like you have entered a forest. The light is dappled, the air is warmer and cleaner, and you immediately feel less frazzled. If libraries could recreate even a small version of what is done here, the effect on our buildings and the people who use them could be immense.

BIOPHILIC DESIGN THROUGH PATTERN AND TEXTURE

Biophilic design need not be executed merely through the use of living greenery. It can also be incorporated into a space via uses of pattern and texture that *suggest* nature.

The standard resource about this concept is *14 Patterns of Biophilic Design: Improving Health and Well-Being in the Built Environment*, written by Terrapin Bright Green, LLC, an environmental consulting and strategic planning firm.

The authors have developead a definition of biophilic design that has become a benchmark for architects and is useful in providing insight into the basics of the concept. They identify three different forms of biophilic design:

1. Putting nature *into* a space, which is the incorporation of plants, water, rocks, wood, air, and light into a specific area. The Ford Foundation atrium, mentioned above, is an example of this.
2. Using natural analogues or substitutes in a space to reference nature more indirectly. These are shapes, forms, and textures that remind you of nature.
3. Using the nature of a space to replicate the feelings or perspectives that you experience in nature and like or appreciate because of our evolution as a species. For example, humans like a sense of danger (not real danger but the thrill that ripples across our nerves when we encounter something that *could* be dangerous). An example of this is the Skywalk, a glass bridge built out over the Grand Canyon, which can be seen below.

Incorporating nature *into* a space, and using the colors, shapes, and materials of nature, are the most obvious ways that libraries can use biophilic design.

IDEAS TO TRY

- **Let in the fresh air.** The simplest and least expensive way of making a space more nature-oriented is to open up doors and windows whenever you can. It is a simple idea, but it can make a real difference in the energy in the library.
- **Create small, tabletop gardens to place around the library. Or, create terrariums using moss.** You can use a bowl, plate, or even a plastic container for a succulent garden. A terrarium can be made from anything that allows the sun in (photosynthesis is what keeps a terrarium active), such as a glass bowl, a small fishbowl, or even a clear glass Christmas ornament.
- **Experiment with incorporating plants into your library's interior design by grouping a number of hardy plants together near existing seating.** The goal is that when someone sits near the plants, they feel like they are in a mini oasis of green. You don't have to create a greenhouse in every area in your library to incorporate biophilic design. Rather, your goal should be to create small, interior parks in your library that make patrons feel they are experiencing the peace and calm of nature.
- **Purchase small tabletop fountains and put them near seating in the library.** The sound of water is wonderfully relaxing and adds to the sense of the outdoors being brought indoors.
- **Use natural light in your library by ensuring there are chairs and/ or tables situated anyplace where there is sunshine or a view of outdoor green spaces.**
  - » Do a review of your library by walking around at different times of the day. Note when spaces have natural sunlight and which windows have good views. Then, consider how to reposition your furniture to take the greatest advantage of both light and views.
  - » For newcomers to your library, create a map identifying which places are best for natural light at which times of day. If your library is located in a cold climate, tell your library users where they can sit to absorb the most sunlight on a cold winter day. This is a public service—seasonal affective disorder (SAD) is caused by lack of sunlight and is a very real thing if you live in the northern part of the country!
- **Experiment by putting natural lightbulbs in defined areas of your library.** Natural light is too bright for some individuals, but others love the clarity and energy it provides. It is also a simple way to bring the outdoors inside.

- **Incorporate a fish tank in your library.** This idea can be very simple (a small goldfish bowl) or complicated (a saltwater aquarium with multiple types of fish). In either case put the tank where people can sit near it and watch the movement of the inhabitants. It is mesmerizing and proven to lower blood pressure, which is why you tend to see fish tanks in doctors' offices.

- **Use color and natural materials to simulate the outdoors and energize a space.** While you might not be able to create a full biophilic environment due to space/financial constraints, you can always use paint and simple houseplants to create a sense of the outdoors. Incorporating natural materials like stone and wood also supports this, as does including shapes that remind you of the outdoors.

- **Incorporate organic shapes into your space through art, furniture, or textiles.** This idea can be as simple or as complex as you want to make it. In the children's area at Curtis Memorial Library, a "tree" was made by a volunteer at the library who enjoyed woodworking and was excited to help create this organic-shaped element. The mural was painted by a local artist. Sun streams into this room in the morning, making it a wonderfully warm and welcoming space for children and their caregivers. Plus, the biophilic components of the room cost nothing, although they

did take time and energy to execute. Also, I will mention that the room was not originally designed to be a biophilic space. It was designed this way because it was fun, it created a pleasant space for families, and it was an agreeable place to spend time. However, it does show the power of this concept.

Another incorporation of biophilic design can also be seen in the same children's play area at Curtis. The children's librarian wanted to create a space for children that was full of energy and movement. In addition to the wooden tree and wall mural, she purchased carpeting for the floor that had wave shapes designed in it. The colors are muted but contribute to the sense of movement and space in the room. This space is one of the most popular in Curtis Library and provides an environment where kids can play, parents can converse, and everyone can feel like they are outside, even on the coldest of Maine days.

- **Plant aromatic indoor gardens in small boxes.** These gardens can be small, but they still pack a punch because their aroma creates a bigger impact than their size might warrant otherwise. Consider plants like geranium, thyme, jasmine, or eucalyptus.
- **Create a moss wall.** A (dry) moss wall is fairly inexpensive and works well in spaces that are not conducive to plant life because of lighting, irrigation, or budgetary concerns. If you are interested in developing a moss wall, consider partnering with a local greenhouse. Your library will benefit from their expertise, and the greenhouse can expand the reach of their services by supporting a very visible project in a high-traffic space like the local library.
  - » Another way to develop a moss wall is to make it a community project. Provide a frame, the glue, and the dried moss. Ask your community to help build the moss wall by adding a piece of moss to the frame whenever they visit the library.
- **Create a living wall that encompasses multiple types of plants.** Living walls are truly breathtaking and attention-grabbing (see photo on following page). They change the energy of any space they inhabit, reducing noise and creating an environment in which people want to spend time. They are also expensive to create and require regular maintenance, so those issues should be considered before starting.
- **Create an indoor water feature.** An indoor water feature has same attributes as a tabletop fountain. It is just bigger and provides a larger focal point in a space. The noise of water is very calming and also tends

to pull people into a space. The statue *The Little Water Girl* is an example of a water feature inside the Portland Public Library in Portland, Maine. It was moved to the library many years ago. When the library was recently renovated, the statue was turned into a focal point in its atrium. The sound of water falling is relaxing and serene, and makes the entry space to Portland Public Library very appealing.

WILL THIS WORK AT MY LIBRARY?

To decide if you want to incorporate biophilic design in your library, consider these questions:

- **Do people spend time in your library? Do they hang out there, meet their friends, chat quietly, knit, read, do crossword puzzles, study?** If the answers to those questions are "no," incorporating more green spaces into your library can be very helpful in increasing your institution's usability as a sought-out meeting space.

- **Are there spaces in your building that are often empty?**
  If so, biophilic design is a wonderful tool for pulling people into under-utilized spaces. Adding plants and comfortable chairs immediately makes a space more attractive and desirable.
- **Do you have spaces for green displays?**
  If you do, bear in mind that one lonely plant sitting on a shelf does not equal biophilic design. You need to be able to create the sense of nature in an inside space. You don't have to turn your entire library into the outdoors, but there does need to be enough organic elements to create a feeling of the presence of nature.
- **Do your employees use up a lot of sick time?**
  This one is subjective in that there are a lot of reasons why employees might be out sick regularly. However, poor air quality often plays a key role in an unhealthy workspace. Green spaces, and the feeling that nature is present in your building, can increase the health of your staff simply by providing cleaner air and a more natural environment.

If you decide to incorporate living greenery into your library, it will need to be well-maintained and loved. If you can't assign a staff person or volunteer or pay an expert to take care of your greenery, don't start this process. There is nothing sadder than dried-out plants starved for water.

Also, plants can be expensive. They can also die for no apparent reason. Set expectations accordingly so that the occasional plant's failure to thrive is seen as part of the process, not a reason to stop everything.

Be prepared for the possibility that staff members may want to green up their workspaces as much as the public would like plants in the public spaces. You may want to set some parameters about the size and type of plants allowed in staff areas to ensure that if it becomes a jungle, it is still a jungle where people can get their work done.

AT THE END OF THE DAY

Nature matters in our lives. Incorporating it into our libraries is a powerful way to make them more attractive and more interesting as spaces where people want to spend time versus being spaces through which our patrons simply pass quickly. And, when people want to spend time in a library, that library immediately becomes more relevant and valuable in their lives.

> In every walk with nature one receives far more than he seeks.
> —JOHN MUIR

IF YOU WANT TO LEARN A BIT MORE

Biophilia by Edward O. Wilson, 1984.

"Biophilic Design Initiative." International Living Future Institute. https://living
-future.org/biophilic-design/

"14 Patterns of Biophilic Design." William Browning, Catherine Ryan, and Joseph
Clancy. www.terrapinbrightgreen.com/reports/14-patterns/#the-patterns

"What is biophilic design, and can it really make you happier and healthier?"
Katharine Schwab. Fast Company. https://www.fastcompany.com/90333072/
what-is-biophilic-design-and-can-it-really-make-you-happier-and-healthier

2

INSTAGRAM BAIT
A PICTURE IS WORTH
A THOUSAND WORDS

reating Instagram bait means developing a space that is unexpectedly interesting, colorful, beautiful, compelling, or just plain fun. The space should lend itself to unusual and intriguing photographs because that is the end goal—to get people to come to this space and have their photograph taken. They will then post those photographs on their Instagram account; hence, Instagram bait.

Today, it is easy to find entrepreneurs who market Instagram rooms. They build a series of rooms in a warehouse or an unused, empty space. They give each room a theme to make it intriguing. People pay to enter the space, explore it, and be able to take photographs that center on each room's theme. While the rooms are completely staged, people still flock to the spaces for the experience and the opportunity to get great pictures and prove they were there. These are also called "selfie factories."

Even museums have tried this idea. Yayoi Kusama, a well-known Japanese artist who loves to use color and shape (particularly polka dots), created "infinity rooms," which are spaces lined with mirrors, art, light, and shapes.

The rooms are part of a movement in art to create experiential art displays in which the observer plays an active role in the creation of the art. The rooms were a huge hit and visited by large numbers of people (over 75,000) when they first opened in New York City in 2017.

At Curtis Library we stumbled into this idea. We didn't create an Instagram-worthy space because we were trying to do that. We were simply looking at our library space, which was very formal and elegant, and asking ourselves, *How do we convey that, yes, this space is beautiful, but also friendly and welcoming?*

One of the library staff members saw a photograph of a street in Spain where every year umbrellas are hung across and up and down the street above people's heads. The result is a beautiful, fun, vibrant splash of color and energy in a totally unexpected place. She came to me with the idea, and we decided to try it.

We purchased approximately thirty colorful umbrellas and asked our building manager how we could go about hanging the umbrellas upside down in a somewhat boring, walk-through space connecting the library's original space to a more recent addition.

The umbrellas went up, and the result was immediate. The space had a whole new level of energy and visual appeal. Our patrons noticed the umbrellas right away and commented on them. They found them to be fun and attractive and started taking pictures of them for social media. We knew we had *arrived* when a young couple walked in the building and asked if they

could have their engagement photo taken in the space with the umbrellas. Of course, we agreed. Curtis Library was now officially Instagram-able.

We decided that the umbrellas couldn't stay up all the time because half the reason people took pictures with them was because they were unexpected. The umbrellas were our springtime experience, but for other times of the year, we needed to find other themes. So, the experiments started.

Some of the other ideas we've tried in the same overhead space have included kites, bicycle wheels, three enormous owl banners created by a Curtis librarian (they were particularly gorgeous; see below), lobster buoys (a must-have in Maine), fluffy clouds made out of coffee filters by a local artist, and, most recently, fish that were created by the library staff.

Each idea has been greeted with great interest by our patrons, although occasionally they have been somewhat puzzled about why something was used in the display (bicycle wheels probably pushed boundaries). However, regardless of whether they "liked" the display, every idea created a new energy in the space, brought people up the stairs to look more closely at the display, and resulted in a new burst of library vitality as people came in to take pictures.

This use of space also made good use of high ceilings that had been empty of anything save some cobwebs. By putting displays in those spaces, we not only created Instagram-worthy spaces but also put to use part of the library that generally went unnoticed. The sight of a high-ceiling space suddenly filled with color and shapes is an amazing energizer and does a great job of conveying the message that this is a vital, interesting place that welcomes you.

IDEAS TO TRY

A key component of successful Instagram bait is having your visual display appear in unexpected places or tell an intriguing story. The surprise or unlikeliness of its appearance is an important part of the attraction. So, you need to look at your library spaces and think about what might work in this way.

- If you have high ceilings or spaces (like an atrium) where there is an opportunity to hang objects, you have an immediate Instagram-ready space. However, if you don't have a space like this, challenge yourself to think like an artist. Could you turn a dark corner or an unused space into something fun? Could you create an Instagram space in a bathroom?
- Think about shapes and colors that are appealing but that may also tell some story about your community or your library. The lobster buoys that we used at Curtis are an obvious way to showcase a Maine library.
  - » Other objects that you might use to create a display:
    - Discarded books
    - Paper flowers in spring
    - Cut-out snowflakes in winter
    - Have kids in the library draw their body outline, color them, cut them out, and hang them

- Hang a display of photos of community members
- Rugs of different sizes, shapes, and colors
- Flags
- Hats
- Musical instruments
- LPs
- Driftwood
- Almost any found object works in this situation. You just need to use your imagination and make sure the display is full of energy. I think the best ideas are those that somehow tell a story about your library or your community. However, Curtis has gotten plenty out of displays that are there *just because*. Sometimes it is fun just to have strange shapes hanging over your head and to see what stories people make up on their own about why they are there.

- Another way to create Instagram bait is to use a wall to create a display, employing the same tools that you would use above. At Curtis Library we have a room that we call the Collaboratory, which is an interactive learning space for all ages, focused on monthly thematic programs that allow library users to explore different topics.

The Collaboratory's themes have varied dramatically, encompassing topics as different as folk stories, genealogy, color, baseball, and sailing. The key thing is that the room is meant to draw in both adults and kids; so, the theme always encompasses light, color, and shapes, in addition to the topic at hand. The result is a space that completely lends itself to photographs.

In the past few years we have had a spring display titled "Bloom" that includes flower bulbs, blooming forsythia, and recorded bird calls. In sun-starved Maine it is a huge hit every March.

The most recent version included a special space created for kids to read in, made of enormous sunflowers crafted by the librarians. The kids loved the space, but we also discovered that adults did too. We found adults regularly in the sunflower reading nook getting their pictures taken because it was so visually inviting and appealing. This was not the goal of the room, but it certainly was a nice added benefit!

None of these ideas have to cost much money. Our original umbrella idea cost about $50, and since we reuse the umbrellas every year, they quickly paid for themselves. Of greater importance is getting the word out to your community about whatever type of display you have created so that people know it is right there in the library, just waiting to be photographed. We use Instagram primarily for this, since the social media service lends itself to visual images, but Facebook is also a great option.

WILL THIS WORK AT MY LIBRARY?

Creating Instagram bait in your library is a good idea if:

- There is someone on your staff who is good at figuring out how to hang weirdly shaped objects quickly. This is a real skill.
- Your library employs people who enjoy the challenge of finding the right objects to create a display. No one can do this every month, but a group of motivated individuals can do it three to four times a year. It helps to have people who see visual opportunity in *found* objects like bicycle wheels because those are guaranteed to be thought-provoking displays, and they are very inexpensive.
- Your library is located in a community with a sense of humor. Sometimes our displays are prettier than others, sometimes they look a bit like a five-year-old created them, and sometimes they are just kind of weird-looking. People need to be able to embrace the craziness of what might show up. Otherwise, you may spend a lot of time explaining your displays.
- Your library's staff will be comfortable with people wandering into your library who may have never been there before, don't know the "rules," and may spend a lot of time taking photographs. You need to have employees who see these people as an opportunity, not a problem.

- Your library has the ability to market your Instagram-space so people who don't typically use the library know it's there. If you don't market the space, those people won't walk in the door to check it out, and then you've lost the reason for creating it.

There are plenty of blogs, articles, and stories about why creating an Instagram-able space is not a good idea. The whole concept of allowing museum visitors to take pictures of artwork *and* include themselves in those pictures has created a heated and intriguing discussion about what is *art* versus *self-indulgence*.

However, if a space is filled with a display that is genuine and an honest part of its environment—and just happens to be a fun place to take pictures—I see an opportunity, not a problem, for libraries. It is interesting, it keeps the library space energized, it gives library staff an opportunity to be really creative, and it can be done very inexpensively.

The biggest downside is that ideas can get complicated and take up too much staff time and energy. There is also the possibility of spending too much on materials for installations in the spirit of *one-upping* the last installation. We avoid that by making *low/no cost* a key element of any display and by using community partners (a local kite enthusiast group did a kite display) whenever possible.

You may wonder what the difference is between a regular library display and an Instagram-worthy display. I think an Instagram display is there for the pure fun of it and to make a space attractive, interesting, and visually unique. A traditional library display is more often meant to educate, inform, or share information. Instagram displays are frivolous in some ways in that they don't have a serious purpose. However, the buzz they create for the library is important and worthwhile. Plus, they are entertaining and foster happiness when you see them!

AT THE END OF THE DAY

Every adult who has used libraries when they were kids (but hasn't used them much since) thinks they know and understand libraries. In their mind a library is the same hushed, quiet space that they visited when they were ten years old.

Creating vibrant, colorful, photo-worthy spaces in your library is a wonderful way to challenge those assumptions and possibly bring people in who haven't been there in a very long time. The unexpected can be very attractive and powerful.

> Unexpected intrusions of beauty. This is what life is.
> —SAUL BELLOW

IF YOU WANT TO LEARN A BIT MORE

"Instagram bait: Why Starbucks put a unicorn meme on its menu." Patrick Kulp. *Mashable*. https://mashable.com/2017/04/23/starbucks-unicorn-frappuccino-chains-instagram-bait/

"Selfie factories: The rise of the made-for-Instagram museum." Arielle Pardes. *Wired*. www.wired.com/story/selfie-factories-instagram-museum/

"12 Awesome Ideas to Create Instagram 'Baits' for Your Event." *Eventplanner*. www.eventplanner.net/news/9349_12-awesome-ideas-to-create-instagram-baits-for-your-event.html

3

ART IN THE BATHROOM
YOU CAN MAKE ANY SPACE BEAUTIFUL

At this point I'm going to take a wild guess and assume you are thinking, *What?!* Generally, we don't seek out public bathrooms for the art in them, and I'm sure most library visitors don't want to spend any more time in the bathroom than absolutely necessary.

However, there is an idea worth considering here. Turn your public bathroom space into something intriguing and different—space that surprises people and creates another point of interest in your building—and you will have developed yet another tool to encourage people to walk into your library (for more than just the obvious uses of a bathroom!) and spend enjoyable time there.

Art museums have been doing art installations in bathrooms for many years. The bathrooms in the Smith College Museum of Art are a wonderful example. The restrooms act as works of art that are quite beautiful. They use tile as the primary medium, but they are also fully functional. As such, they encourage you to consider concepts like the blurring between public and private space and form versus function. Ellen Driscoll and Sandy Skoglund, both of whom are well-known artists outside the bathroom genre, created the spaces.

These bathrooms were, in turn, inspired by the bathroom art at the John Michael Kohler Arts Center in Sheboygan, Wisconsin. These washrooms were begun in 1974 as a way of giving artists access to the technology and materials developed by Kohler Co., and of providing a venue for them to explore how those materials could be used in works of combined art/industry.

Another example of bathrooms as art instillations can be found in the public bathroom in Kawakawa, a small town in New Zealand. The bathrooms were designed by New Zealand artist and architect Friedensreich Hundertwasser, using recycled materials such as bottles and tiles embedded in rough, industrial concrete. A living tree grows up through the roof of the washrooms as an added feature. While not as traditionally *artistic* as the Smith or Kohler bathrooms, the Kawakawa bathrooms have a very intriguing look that has brought many people into the community to visit.

The Grassroots Art Center in Lucas, Kansas, is another organization that has an *arty* bathroom concept, albeit a bit different in design than the above examples. The art center is dedicated to the idea of supporting grassroots art, which focuses particularly on the use of recycled items. The entrance to the bathroom on the outside of the building is shaped like an enormous toilet bowl. It uses recycled materials in a mosaic that includes almost everything but the kitchen sink: plates, bottles, bottle tops, and found items. It puts the art in place before you walk into the bathroom but is nonetheless effective in creating a show-stopping idea.

Yes, people come into public libraries regularly just to use the facilities. However, all of the above ideas show the power of using art in a bathroom setting. It certainly is different and intriguing (*Why did the organization do this*? patrons may wonder) and encourages discussion.

IDEAS TO TRY

- Ask artists in your community if they would be interested in doing a permanent installation in some or all of your bathrooms or involving the entrance to your bathrooms. The value to the artist is obvious in that he or she will get a *lot* of exposure (in more ways than one!). Obviously, artists that want a more highbrow audience probably won't like this idea, but there are a lot of smart, savvy new artists who would see the value of the concept.

- Your library could also turn this into a community project. Provide kids (of any age) with washable paint and a theme and ask them to give a bathroom an artistic flair. Then, see what happens. If it is awful, it doesn't have to be permanent, but you might just be happy with the end result.
- If you have a college or university in your town, you could ask the art professors about developing a program/class centered around creating a public art project out of your bathrooms.
- Create photo exhibits or small art exhibits in your bathrooms.
- Change the lighting in bathrooms regularly and create a different environment that way.
- Put tactile art in your public bathrooms in the form of mobiles or origami.
- Hang book art or hang shelves on which book art could be placed.
- Create an installation in a bathroom of give-away art. This could be in the form of bookmarks or book art or collages—anything that incorporates creative expression and permits the observer to walk away with the art if they like it enough.

WILL THIS WORK AT MY LIBRARY?

If you want your library to become less transactional and more experiential, a bathroom art show might be just the way to go. The idea certainly inspires discussion, questions, and interaction.

You might even want to have staff members willing to be docents and answer questions about the art if you get a lot of people walking into your library to see the installation. I would personally go out of my way to see a bathroom at a library with an art installation, out of curiosity if nothing else.

Art in the bathroom is also a wonderful public relations tool, and, if you feel some may consider the idea a bit too crazy for your library, you can simply cite examples of such displays already in place at major institutions to give the idea some gravitas.

If you have staff at your library who enjoy chatting with library users, the bathroom idea can work. If your librarians are more interested in getting the work done than talking to people about those crazy bathrooms, this idea is most likely a bit too much. Having a staff with a great sense of humor would also be very helpful.

From a space perspective I think this idea works best if you have unisex bathrooms. Otherwise, if you get really great art in the bathroom, eventually you may have women in the men's room because they want to see the art displayed there, and vice versa. If the bathrooms are unisex, everyone will have the opportunity to visit all of the art.

The idea of *bathroom as a destination* may seem a bit scary to those of us who spend a lot of time making sure our bathrooms don't become dens of iniquity.

However, it is exactly because bathrooms in public spaces can be problematic that I like this idea. Author Malcolm Gladwell wrote a very intriguing book in 2002 titled *The Tipping Point*. The core idea in the book is that very small things can *tip* a situation one way or another in terms of how people respond to it.

Gladwell uses the example that when a subway in a city gets a small piece of graffiti on it, it should be dealt with immediately. Otherwise, people will see that graffiti, and its presence sends a message that no one is taking care of the problem. So, people must not care about the space. Therefore, it is okay to create more graffiti. And that is how urban wastelands start.

By the same token, the reverse is also true. If you take care of small things like bathrooms, by putting art in those places, it becomes obvious that someone cares. So, if a bathroom has art in it, people are more likely to not disrupt that space because the space is being used and has value (beyond the obvious).

I don't know if this would work in real life versus theory, but I like the concept, and it makes sense to me. It certainly is worth an experiment. Perhaps a *destination bathroom* in a library might keep those spaces clean and free of problems. We haven't tried this idea yet at Curtis, but I would like to at least experiment with some of the simpler versions to see what happens.

AT THE END OF THE DAY

The power of art to attract people's attention can't be disputed. With some creativity and a little bit of humor, you can invest unexpected spaces in your library with that power.

> Art is everywhere you look for it.
> —EL GRECO

IF YOU WANT TO LEARN A BIT MORE

"Bowl Plaza." Grassroots Art Center. www.grassrootsart.net/bowl-plaza

"Loo with a view: 10 public bathrooms that are works of art." Jan Schroder. www.fodors.com/news/photos/loo-with-a-view-10-public-bathrooms-that -are-works-of-art

"Museum restrooms as functional art." Smith College. www.smith.edu/bfac/ restrooms.php

"Washrooms." John Michael Kohler Arts Center. https://www.jmkac.org/ exhibitions/collections/washrooms-new.html

4

LAB STORES
TESTING, TESTING, TESTING

T esting, testing, and testing again was the mantra for many years when companies were developing new products. It was not uncommon for product development to take one to two years before a product finally got to market. The tests were expensive and consumed a lot of resources. If the product bombed when it finally got to market, it was a big loss to a company.

Today, many companies are taking a different approach to product and service development. They want more realistic testing and to be able to test a lot of different ideas in a short period of time, and they don't want to risk a huge amount of money in the process.

From these demands came the idea of lab stores, or as they are otherwise known, "experiential test sites." These are brick-and-mortar stores that provide the opportunity for retailers to test out new concepts, products, and services in an actual store with actual customers.

Lab stores are very useful for analyzing potential shopping environments and for exposing customers to new products and services to get their input.

Most retailers would prefer to test in a real-world situation because consumers respond in a more realistic way than if they are in an obvious test environment.

Even huge stores such as Walmart tests ideas and concepts with their customers. Recently, they opened a test retail store called the Intelligent Retail Lab (IRL). The store is focused on using artificial intelligence (AI) to help manage inventory, with over one hundred servers in use in the store to support the enterprise. There are also some fun technology bells and whistles in Walmart's IRL, such as a digital screen that customers can interact with by using their bodies (the screen reflects what the person in front of it is doing in a stylized fashion). Customers can also use interactive, end-of-aisle display units to search for items or get information about products.

Another example of a lab store can be seen at 7-Eleven, the convenience store. Their lab store has indoor and outdoor seating and features craft food/drink, as well as a simplified self-checkout process that allows customers to use their telephones to scan and go. These tests help 7-Eleven evaluate new ways of serving customers, reducing costs, and delivering food and drink that may not fit into the traditional expectations of what the company provides.

Bed Bath & Beyond opened twenty-one next-generation lab stores in 2018 to test new concepts in product offerings, store designs, and inventory management. The stores have been very successful in helping the company understand both the products that customers want to find when they walk in the door and how they shop the store. In an age when fewer customers use retail stores in favor of the internet, the test stores have provided invaluable knowledge for Bed Bath & Beyond as they seek to stay relevant.

IDEAS TO TRY

Libraries are perfect experiential test sites. They have patrons of all ages and from all demographics walking into the building every day. Those patrons generally have a great deal of ownership in what happens at the library and are usually more than happy to tell you what they think about any new developments in the library space. All you have to do is start using your space as a lab store and start asking questions.

- Declare a specific day of the week as your library's *Testing Tuesday* or *Feedback Friday* in the library. Put a sign on or by your front door so your patrons know that testing is going on that day at the library.

> » Try a new service and ask for feedback about that service in real time. For example, you could provide a new readers' advisory service in the library and ask for input from anyone who tries the service.
> » Or, you could set up a special kiosk or desk by an entrance and talk to visitors as they walk in your door.

- Put a test idea into place in your library, *don't* label it as a test, and observe what happens. If the idea doesn't work, it is easy to pull it and move on to the next idea. If patrons notice and use the service, you can expand and build upon it.
  > » The only difficulty with this approach is figuring out how long to keep a test idea in the library before deciding whether it is or isn't working. To address this, before you start the test identify how long the test will run. Sticking to a timetable will help avoid tests that drift on forever.

- Changing how a space is used can be problematic in a library where patrons are used to things that have always remained the same. Try picking one or two spaces in your library, make them your test spaces, and don't expand beyond that to start. Your patrons will get comfortable over time with the idea that spaces can have multiple uses, and then you can begin to expand your test ideas into other spaces if that is useful.
  > » We have one room at Curtis that, over time and depending on need and the tests we are implementing, has been used as an early-morning pre-opening space, a financial literacy education room, a room with vending machines and tables for eating, and a room that contains our best sellers and new books. We have changed the function of this room so often that by the time we started changing other spaces to test ideas, we barely heard a peep from our library patrons.

- Don't forget that when asking questions, gathering feedback, or just trying out a new service, you can use your virtual space as another type of lab store. Set up a schedule for sending out questions to your community on Facebook and/or your website. A schedule makes it easier for patrons to know when you are going to ask for their feedback, and many people who enjoy giving feedback will make a point of remembering that schedule.

Several years ago, Curtis Library wanted to get feedback for our strategic plan update. Using an idea created for the Miami-Dade Public Library System in 2014, we developed a plan for feedback called "10 days, 100 great ideas." Over a ten-day period, we posted questions for our community on Facebook and our website and asked for input.

By the end of the ten-day period, we had received over 1,500 ideas from the community that were extremely helpful with respect to our strategic plan. Many people started answering questions on day one of the project and came back to answer questions every day for the next nine days because they enjoyed the idea so much.

WILL THIS WORK AT MY LIBRARY?

A lab store (virtual or physical) makes sense if your library tries out new ideas regularly and needs a way to determine if you want to scale an idea to the full library or library system.

However, lab stores can take energy and work to develop in any format. It is very easy to get so involved in creating a test (should we ask a question this way or that way?) that you lose sight of the objective, which is to obtain feedback. It is important to develop a clear focus on what you need to know and not get diverted by the "it would be nice to know" syndrome.

Two key reasons why lab stores are useful are because they are real life and because anything that is done can be easily undone. You do not want to test an idea and then feel like you have to implement it because it was so expensive to test. If that is the case, you aren't testing; you are introducing a new idea. Make sure your tests are fast, inexpensive, and don't pull you into the black hole of "you tested this idea so now you have to do it." Having test spaces should help you move quickly so you can explore multiple ideas and find the winners. As any entrepreneur will tell you, failing fast, failing cheap, and failing often is a very good way to find the best ideas without going bankrupt in the process.

AT THE END OF THE DAY

Libraries of all types are testing, exploring, and innovating every day to find new ways to deliver what our communities want. Keep in mind that you don't have to do big, expensive tests of your ideas that require a lot of people and time to make them happen. Think about how you can use your library space to test ideas, and remember that the person who fails the most . . . wins.

> **Quality is never an accident;**
> **it is always the result of intelligent effort.**
> —JOHN RUSKIN

IF YOU WANT TO LEARN A BIT MORE

"At Walmart's Intelligent Retail Lab, the future is here." Michael Browne. *Supermarket News*. www.supermarketnews.com/retail-financial/walmart-s-intelligent-retail-lab-future-here

"7-Eleven unveils 'lab' store." Marianne Wilson. *Chain Store Age*. www.chainstoreage.com/store-spaces/7-eleven-unveils-lab-store/

"Walmart just opened a 50,000-square-foot store of the future – see inside." Dennis Green. *Business Insider*. www.businessinsider.com/walmart-opens-intelligent-retail-lab-store-of-the-future-2019-4

5

HALLWAY HANGOUTS
USE THE SPACE BETWEEN SPACES

Have you ever heard the expression "life is a journey, not a destination"? Using the space between spaces is something like that. As architects have started to tune in more to the concept of people-oriented spaces versus theoretical concept-oriented spaces, they have begun to realize that a lot happens in the *empty* places that go from one space to another. And what happens is powerful.

People stop to have conversations with each other. Hallway discussions sometimes turn into brainstorming sessions right there. People sit in a hallway space and think and gather ideas. People sit down at a desk in an otherwise empty walk-through space and start to work.

Because of this recognition of how people work and interact, smart people have started developing furniture and equipment that work specifically in the between spaces. Movable chairs and tables have started to appear in hallways and corners, allowing people to either work on their own or get together in a group with others. Academic institutions started putting whiteboards in hallways so that informal communication could be formalized and written down.

In their article "'Smart' Spaces Aren't Just for Classrooms Anymore," American architects Darren L. James and Nestor Infanzon called the between places "serendipity spaces" because so much informal creativity and connection happened in them.

If you grew up in the '60s or '70s, you are probably comfortable going into a very quiet room, sitting down, and working in absolute silence. That is what baby boomers learned was the way to get work done.

However, if you are a Gen Xer or millennial, the odds are good that you have a totally different approach to getting your work done. You are used to working in short bursts, accessing the internet as your key resource. You are perfectly okay with interruptions and music or noise, and in fact you might seek them out because too much prolonged focus on one activity doesn't work for you. You are actually drawn to work in the between spaces.

Libraries, because they serve individuals at both ends of the above demographic spectrum, must have spaces that work for everyone. However, most libraries are large buildings that were not designed to be flexible to meet different types of needs. Users were expected to adapt to the building, not the other way around.

Imagine how much more space you would have for all of your library users of every type if you considered every corner, hallway, and empty space between and found a way to turn them into comfortable, inviting, flexible spaces that could appeal to anyone and everyone? Suddenly, your big old library starts to have more possibilities.

If you can turn even some of those between places into a space that welcomes every passerby to sit down, relax, chat, or do work, you immediately increase the likelihood of people spending more time in your library. The more time people spend in the library, the less transactional their interaction becomes, and the more people feel like they are part of a real community. That is what makes between spaces a very useful tool for libraries.

One of my favorite places at Curtis Library is a green between space. (How's that for a good example of combining ideas?!) Our original library building, built in 1904, is connected to our 1999 addition via the use of a mezzanine with a glass skylight. The space was never used for anything other than as a passage from one building to the other and was very static until we started using the space to try out several projects.

One of those projects was to turn the mezzanine into a between space, which I took to calling the "mezzanine green." The idea was to turn the space into a comfortable front-porch type of space, where library patrons could sit and enjoy the sun that comes through the glass skylight. We added wicker chairs and tables and then started creating the green space by adding plants, plants, and more plants. The result feels like a Victorian greenhouse and has become one of the most popular places in the library to work, chat, or just sit. People love the fact that they can be part of the library's energy without having to be in the middle of it.

Another example of how between spaces can be put to use can be found at Curtis' neighbor in Brunswick: Bowdoin College. Several years ago, the Bowdoin Library decided to add a media commons. Rather than build out an entirely new building, the library got creative with the space it already had available. An underground passage that went from the original library to their newer building became the core of the new commons. The space was typical of a transitional space—empty and not particularly useful. However, once carpeting was put in and chairs and tables added, rooms off the passage became screening rooms, and suddenly an old space had a new, useful life.

IDEAS TO TRY

- Visit a nearby academic institution. Colleges are becoming experts in developing between spaces because their students are experts in finding empty spaces that they can plunk down in and start using. Look at the furniture and equipment in hallways and pass-through spaces and notice how students use them.
- Put two comfortable chairs and a small table between them in a hallway or connecting space in your library. Make the space attractive by providing some sort of lamp for good lighting and possibly add a plant. Keep watch and see how long it takes before people start sitting there, either individually or together to have a chat. If no one ever sits there, try another space until you find a space that works for your library users.
- Try the same idea but equip the space for innovation, brainstorming, and teamwork. This can be as simple as putting up a whiteboard on a wall with a table and chairs nearby that can be moved if people want to work with the whiteboard.
- Put wheels on a few tables and chairs in your library and signs on them that tell people to please use that furniture wherever is most comfortable for them. Take note of where they end up most often. Move tables and chairs there for regular use.
- Don't assume that people will not want to sit and work in a between space. Recently, we needed to move our station for library volunteers out of the office, where it had been located for years. The volunteer coordinator and building manager decided to create a bigger and more comfortable volunteer station in a between space—the hallway that goes from a basement meeting space to the main atrium in the library (see photo on following page). I was afraid the volunteers would feel like they weren't getting an important enough space in the library and would be insulted. Instead, with a bit of care and attention to making the space attractive and useful, they loved their new location.
- Between spaces don't always have to be in a hallway. Consider how you might restructure your library stacks to create more spaces for your patrons. Like most public libraries, over the past ten years Curtis has reduced the size of its paper reference collection. As a result, we were able to take down some shelving to create new spaces in which we put tables and chairs so people could sit and read or study. We also added a stand-alone, movable display stand as a way of sharing library information in a between space.

WILL THIS WORK AT MY LIBRARY?

Staff members at your library need to be flexible enough to deal with between-space users who might not follow the traditional rules of a library. For example, they might want to drink their coffee or eat in places where such activities were not allowed in the past. They might want to talk on their cellphone. They might want to have a chat with their neighbor. You might find that a group of students has taken over a space to have a study group. Chairs and tables might get moved to meet the specific needs of individuals. Are all of those new ways of using the library okay? You will need to figure out new ways to manage spaces that keep some of the norms that traditional library users want while opening up new spaces.

Beyond the need for flexibility, I don't see many issues around the idea of creating between spaces, but I have received some negative feedback from patrons as I've done this work at Curtis Library. I'll share them here, and you can decide if they are problems your library may encounter or not:

- **Feedback:** Putting chairs, furniture, and other useful tools into between spaces can clutter up a library. The library's architect designed the space to create a specific impression. If you put something in that space that wasn't meant to be there in the first place, you have ruined the feeling that the architect was trying to create.
  - » **Response:** I think libraries are best when they are treated as living entities that change and morph over time to meet the needs of those who walk into them. I adore clean, simple architectural spaces and find them very appealing. However, essentially, the cleaner and neater a space is, the less likely it is to have people in it because people are messy, creative, and unique and want things their way, not yours. I want a library that invites people in and encourages them to sit down and stay a while, and if that means they move the chairs around a bit to make things more comfortable, I am just fine with that.
- **Feedback:** It is expensive to create between spaces. You have to find furniture that works, and we don't have the money for that, nor do we have the staff to do that type of work.
  - » **Response:** No money or available staff are probably the two issues that libraries face with respect to every project they start. It is a fact of life for many libraries. However, if you want to try this idea, just do it, even if it means you are personally moving stuff around your library to make it happen. Success breeds success. If you put a few chairs around a table in a sunny patch of hallway and people start sitting there, you have an argument for doing more with between spaces. In this situation you are creating something that is good for your library's users *and* for the library. It is definitely worth trying it at the nickel and dime level and then expanding from there, because I can almost guarantee people will love it.

AT THE END OF THE DAY

There is value in empty space. However, there is also value in *using* empty space and making it valuable. You need to decide what works at your library and for your library users.

> Music is the space between the notes.
> —CLAUDE DEBUSSY

IF YOU WANT TO LEARN A BIT MORE

"Learning Spaces – In-Between Spaces." Young Office. www.youngoffice.com/solutions/education/learning-spaces-in-between-spaces/

"The Spaces In Between: Where the Next Big Ideas Emerge." Connie Tam. www.globalfurnituregroup.com/insight/spaces-in-between

6

STRATEGY AMPLIFYING SPACES
SHARING WHO YOU ARE
THROUGH YOUR BUILDING

S pace can be an important tool to reflect and reinforce organizational strategy and values. If a company espouses openness and transparency, a space with closed-off perspectives and hard-to-find offices with windowless doors doesn't do a good job of reflecting those ideals. However, a small start-up company seeking to establish itself as innovative, fast-moving, and flexible can help further that perspective as representative of its values by having a corporate space that is eclectic, fun, open, and energetic.

Space designers for corporations start their work by evaluating organizations across multiple characteristics to understand what type of space would work best for that organization, given its personality and values. Some examples of these attributes include *temporality*, which is the degree to which people linger in a space, or *exposure*, which is the degree to which people can expect privacy in speaking or talking on the telephone.

Other attributes may focus on employee wellness. If this is a core value, the organization's spaces might use organic design materials and provide opportunities for employees to work and meet standing up. There may be spaces reserved for employee meditation or workout opportunities. Natural light may be identified as important since it supports alertness and energy.

A consistent and powerful example of using space to reflect organizational values can be seen in the Google corporate headquarters in Mountain View, California. Google's stated mission is to "organize the world's information and make it accessible." Innovative technology is the core component of achieving that mission. The Googleplex (Google's campus) reflects *innovation* and the Google colors everywhere you look. There are odd works of art, like a life-size T. rex skeleton surrounded by plastic pink flamingos. There are stacks of extra-large Rubik's cubes on top of desks that say "Google" on them. There are bicycles painted in the Google brand colors. There are computer desks lined with lava lamps in the Google colors. The entire campus was designed to mirror and amplify the corporation's mission and values, reinforcing them at every opportunity.

Another example of using space design to reflect corporate values is the Etsy headquarters in Brooklyn, New York. Etsy's core values include crafts, community support, social innovation, and sustainability. Hanging from the ceiling in the building's lobby are large, colored-paper and wood-design elements that reflect the handmade aesthetic of the organization. Biophilic design is used throughout the building, with plants placed everywhere and

workspaces crafted from natural materials. There are collaborative spaces throughout the building and random art displays. Not as visible but equally representative of the company's values, the building has received certification for zero waste. Clearly, there has been a careful focus on using the corporate headquarters as a tool to reinforce the articulation of the company's dedication to crafts.

IDEAS TO TRY

- Review your library's mission, vision, and values. Think about how you can convey those values visually. For example, many libraries today work to foster community. How can you say *community* the minute people walk in the library's doors? A community is welcoming, so there needs to be cheerful faces and smiles. Consider putting up a sign or banner that simply says "Welcome." Put casual seating throughout the library to encourage people to sit and chat with each other. All of those things help say *community*.

- Don't be afraid to challenge the sacred cows at your library to make sure your space tells the right story. I interviewed a senior executive from L.L.Bean several years ago. We talked about customer service as a core value and how you share that value with people walking in your front door. As I walked him downstairs to the front door on his way out of the library, he casually mentioned to me that the security gates at both of the library's main entrances didn't exactly support the concepts of *welcome* and *community*. At first, I brushed off that comment, since of course a library has to have security gates! Then, as I thought more about his comment, I realized he was right. It took some time to move everyone to the same perspective, but ultimately we took down the library's security gates, and I think our entrance is infinitely more welcoming and open as a result. I know this idea may not work everywhere, but it did here, and I can happily report that we still have basically the same number of books that we have always had!

- Do you still want your library to say "books" the minute people walk in the door? Many libraries designed their entry spaces so that the first thing you see when you walk into the library is the lending services desk. This made sense at one point in time, since everything in the library revolved around books and lending those books to the community.
  » Today's library still prizes books, but we also value many other things. How do we convey that (without losing those who love

books and reading) in our spaces? What about moving your lending desk, so it no longer takes up all of the initial physical and visual space when people enter the library? You could replace the desk with public space for meeting, working, and providing ad hoc programming. That would do more to reflect today's library and still maintain the connection to our past that is relevant and important.

- Don't forget the simple way of sharing your mission, vision, and values through graphics. Post your values in a prominent place in the library so that your users can see them every time they walk in the doors of the library. At Curtis Library we have banners hanging outside the building that articulate one of our most important beliefs: "You are welcome here." We also have banners that encourage people to experience the library in the way that works best for them. "Read, play, create. It's your library, you decide."

- Another way to reflect your library's values is to incorporate quotes. At Curtis we created enormous bookmarks with quotes that reinforce our branding and the value that we place in reading (see photo on following page).

- Color is another important way to frame spaces to a specific message. At Curtis the library architects developed a gray color scheme that was very soothing and quiet and was perfect in a traditional library space.

» However, after a new library wing was built in 1999, the library started to evolve into a more vibrant, busy, louder place. When the library's brand was updated in 2007, we asked the brand designers to develop a color palette that would work with the existing gray palette but that would have more energy and vibrancy. As we have needed to paint in the library, we have incorporated those colors, with the result that our colors now support our mission (community) and how our library is used. The colors also pop nicely throughout the library because we use them judiciously.

• If you aren't sure about the message people are receiving when they walk into your library, ask your users how the entrances to the library make them feel. Welcome? Informed? Entertained? As they walk around the building, do their feelings change? Do they feel more welcome in some areas than others? Where are you doing things right, and where can you make changes?

WILL THIS WORK AT MY LIBRARY?

This idea only works if your library, staff, and board have a very clear understanding of your institutional mission and your values. You can't create a space to reflect these things if you don't have a laser-sharp focus on what they are.

You can use space to reflect strategy and values very simply and inexpensively via the use of signs articulating these elements. Or, you can go all the way and use building design elements/features the way Google and Etsy have done. This is obviously much more expensive.

However, the inexpensive process is still a good option because it allows you to change regularly the promotional tool that you are using and that helps keep community awareness current about your message. For example, every time we put new banners in the library, our patrons see them very quickly and absorb the message. Without that regular change, people stop *seeing* building elements fairly quickly, and the concept becomes ineffective. I also like the fact that regular change requires regular reviews of strategy, and that helps keep it fresh in the minds of everyone who works at the library.

This idea is also a good one if you are able to look at your library space as a whole, identify three or four elements that can support your strategy, and then use those consistently throughout your building. Some examples of elements might include color, lighting, or furniture. That way, each time someone encounters those elements in any part of your building, the message about strategy is being reinforced and repeated. If you can't do this consistently, the danger is that one message is being conveyed in one location but not in another.

AT THE END OF THE DAY

People want to do business with organizations that are clear about *how* they do business and *what* they provide. If your space is a reflection of your organization's values, it makes it easy for potential users to make a determination if they want to use your brand.

> When your values are clear to you,
> making decisions becomes easier.
> —ROY E. DISNEY

IF YOU WANT TO LEARN A BIT MORE

"How Corporate Culture Influences Workplace Design." Susan Foong, John Chapman. HGA. https://hga.com/aligning-corporate-culture-and-workplace-design/

"How We Designed a Studio Space That Reflects Our Values." Juho Parviainen. IDEO. www.ideo.com/blog/how-we-designed-a-studio-space-that-reflects-our-values

"Morningstar Offices – Chicago." Office Snapshots. https://officesnapshots.com/2017/02/28/morningstar-offices-chicago/

7

EXPERIENCES
DON'T LET ME GET BORED
WHEN I WALK IN YOUR DOOR

Today, retailers face the constant dilemma of shopper boredom. How do you keep people visiting a brick-and-mortar retail store, particularly when the internet can provide almost anything you want, when you want it, and how you want it? If a store looks the same over two or three visits and can't compete with the fluidity of the online environment, a retailer runs the very real risk of shoppers zoning out—literally.

Regular reinvention of what a retail space looks and feels like is a powerful tool to keep people walking in the doors. Many people shop for entertainment. Other people shop for utility. In both cases if you can create an interesting environment for the shopper every time they walk in, a retailer has a good point of difference, allowing it to stand out from its competition and ensure steady traffic.

The concept store Story, located across from the High Line in Manhattan, opened in 2011. Until the store was bought out by Macy's in 2018, it was completely reinvented every four to eight weeks with a new design and new products and marketing.

The founder, Rachel Shechtman, defined the concept in the Good Life Project podcast by saying it "takes the point of view of a magazine, changes like a gallery and sells things like a store . . . Story completely reinvents itself—from merchandise and store design to floor plan and fixtures—to bring to light a new theme, trend, or issue." The concept is successful. Sales equals those of the top retailers in the world on a per-square-foot basis.

Story was obviously an outlier with respect to how often it changed its retail environment. It is very challenging to change a store every two to three years, much less every four to eight weeks! Urban Outfitters pursues the same strategy as Story but not on such a short timeframe. Urban Outfitters is known for its willingness to experiment with store design using art displays and temporary pop-ups as a way of calling attention to their products and apparel.

Creating experiential spaces is another way retailers keep their spaces new, fresh, and exciting. Manufacturers like L.L.Bean create instore shopping experiences that allow customers to try before they buy. They can put on hiking boots and try them out on an artificial hill. They can get a fly-casting rod and take a quick one-hour course on how to use the rod out on the lawn at an L.L.Bean store. Their Freeport, Maine, store offers a huge aquarium filled with trout so shoppers can see up close what they are trying to catch. There is even a trout pond inside the L.L.Bean headquarters in Freeport, Maine, that grabs the attention of every shopper. All of these activities make it fun and different every time a consumer walks in the door, thereby eliminating shopper boredom.

HOW CAN MY LIBRARY TRY THIS IDEA?

It is challenging to create new, exciting experiences for shoppers, even for retailers who have the staff, funding, and expertise to do so. For librarians, the idea of constantly having to reinvent the library as a whole most likely seems overwhelming.

However, I do think it is possible to create *a space* in the library that changes regularly and creates energy and excitement for anyone visiting the library. At Curtis Library we decided to move a public computer lab from the first floor to the second, closer to the adult services desk. The result was a large, empty space on the first floor of the library in the middle of the building.

After a lot of research and staff discussion about how we might use that space, we decided to turn it into the Curtis Collaboratory, an interactive learning space for all ages. The idea was based on the interactive displays found at science museums, as well as on the Idea Box at the Oak Park Public Library.

Essentially, each month we create a new theme and develop learning activities to go with that theme. Some examples include programs about color, baseball, our local history, genealogy, folk tales, writing, flowers, theater, and sailing. Each display includes books from our book collection that supports the theme, activities for kids and adults, videos to watch, and comfortable seating. Often, we have speakers or performers to entertain patrons within the space. Our goal has been to offer something new on a regular basis for our patrons to explore and enjoy. The changeover from one month to the next has become a point of excitement for local children, who now run into the library to discover the newest theme.

The Idea Box at Oak Park Library has displays and programs similar to those at Curtis but it also explores social justice issues (*What comes out of restorative justice?*), community feedback is requested (*What kind of community do you want to live in?*), and the library's special collections are put on display for the community.

The Charlotte Mecklenburg Library in Mecklenburg, North Carolina, has created an idea box that inspires patrons to get creatively messy in the form of a makerspace, which has available 3D printers, CAD stations, vinyl and laser cutters, sewing machines, and other technologies that allow creators to go from brainstorming to design to the actual creation of ideas.

IDEAS TO TRY

The above examples of creation spaces take a great deal of time and planning.

- A simpler way to build a creation space would be to develop a site in your library that focuses on problem-solving. Identify a community or library problem. Provide sticky notes for the community to respond to the question. Change the query every week. The responses will become a source of interest to your community, and because they change consistently, they will help keep the library space fresh and interesting.
- Another experiment would be to have a community art space in the library. This could be as small as a table with one or two chairs. Every week you could provide a simple art project for people to work on. Ask people to leave their creation behind as part of the community project. Again, regular change in a space is fun, creative, and invigorating, as well as great for community building.

WILL THIS WORK AT MY LIBRARY?

Creating an experiential, constantly changing space takes a firm commitment to come up with new ideas month after month and to figure out how to share those ideas in a creative, enticing way in your library. This has worked at Curtis Library because the entire staff supported the idea and was willing to take on the responsibility at one point of time or another to make our Collaboratory work.

However, if you get your community involved in managing an idea room, it makes it more possible. You could ask for volunteers to run the room, identify what is interesting to the community (*Art? Community issues? Lifelong learning?*), and develop a regular calendar of events accordingly.

Over time the idea can also start to cost money. As you learn more about what works in terms of lighting and display and the use of color and imagery, you naturally want to do more, and doing more usually costs more. Because the Curtis Collaboratory does so much around children's themes, it was a natural connection to make it the focus of fundraising for our youngest group of library donors, the Curtis Contemporaries, many of whom are young parents. This helped us address the need for funding.

It can also take a long time for your community to figure out what your space is all about (especially because it changes regularly) and whether they want to take part in it. For a long period of time adults thought the Curtis Collaboratory was just for kids, and they would go out of their way to avoid walking through it!

However, I now have adults often tell me how much they enjoy the changing exhibits and having something new to explore and experience when they come to the library. That alone helped prove to me the idea that an experiential, changing space can do a great deal to keep foot traffic numbers up and encourage people to look at your library less as a point of transaction and more as a destination.

AT THE END OF THE DAY

For decades libraries didn't change because they didn't need to change. People knew what they could find at the library, and libraries were valued.

However, people today want *new*—new experiences, new ideas, new information, new entertainment. Libraries have to figure out how they can change and become more fluid to meet the demand for new. The entire library does not need to change completely to meet such expectations from our patrons, but we do need to show that we understand what people want and demonstrate that we can provide that on a regular basis.

> If you do what you've always done,
> you'll get what you've always gotten.
> —TONY ROBBINS

IF YOU WANT TO LEARN A BIT MORE

Charlotte-Mecklenburg Idea Box. www.cmlibrary.org/idea-box
Oak Park Public Library Idea Box. https://oppl.org/use-your-library/idea-box/
"7 Case Studies That Prove Experiential Retail Is the Future." *Storefront Magazine*. www.thestorefront.com/mag/7-case-studies-prove-experiential -retail-future/

POP-UP SPACES
TELL ME SOMETHING INTERESTING

P op-up spaces are everywhere today. Chefs create pop-up dining experiences in unique locations. Artists have pop-up art installations. Retailers have in-store, pop-up events to celebrate and focus on specific brands. Nonprofit organizations have pop-up events to draw attention to their causes.

Why are they so popular? Pop-ups are seemingly spontaneous, creative, novelty events. Knowing that a pop-up is happening and attending it demonstrate that you are *in the know*. There is a sense of exclusivity in knowing about or going to a pop-up, and that helps make them intriguing.

Some interesting examples of pop-ups:

- IKEA created a pop-up café in Toronto that sold its well-known meatballs and other food that is normally only available in its regular stores. As part of the event, shoppers could also try out kitchen products sold by IKEA that are not as well-known as the company's furniture.

- Pantone created a pop-up during Paris Fashion Week. It provided food in multiple colors that matched its brand colors, thereby providing a focus on its core business while offering a trendy food element product.
- West elm stores have a program called LOCAL. They provide space for in-store pop-ups focused on local artisans and small businesses. Their goal is to celebrate makers across America. They provide added support by incorporating local makers' products on their website.
- A company called Nomad is a mobile fashion boutique in a truck that allows the owner to move to new, pop-up locations at the turn of a key.
- In England Penguin Books joined with a retail shop (Whistles) to create a pop-up library by filling the store with books (and other things for sale).
- Grey Goose Vodka has created a pop-up traveling martini bar (with only two chairs!) in a truck that can be moved from location to location.
- Public libraries have experimented with the pop-up idea, trying out traveling libraries in various places, such as bicycles, electric vans, Little Free Libraries, old telephone booths, and repurposed newspaper dispensers.

Libraries have long offered pop-ups in remote locations in the form of a bookmobile. Today, pop-ups arrive on bicycle, electric carts, wheelbarrows, and sometimes even by horseback. Curtis Library serves a lobstering and fishing community located on three peninsulas. To get books into the hands of folks who can't always make the twenty-five-minute drive into town, we do a pop-up every week at the town offices for the community. We also take our traveling library into local retirement communities, where the residents are not very mobile and greatly appreciate having the reading materials delivered to them.

IDEAS TO TRY

- The easiest pop-up is a Little Free Library (LFL). The concept has been tried successfully across the country, and there is a high awareness in communities about the benefits of LFLs, which include promoting reading and helping to create community by giving neighbors an informal place to stop and chat and get to know each other.
  - » At Curtis Library we have supported the LFL movement by getting local businesses to pay for the raw materials needed for these mini libraries. The materials were cut into the appropriate-sized pieces

by the local vocational/technical school and made available for free at a build-out event at the library. Today, there are sixteen registered LFLs in Brunswick and probably another ten unregistered libraries. They have proven to be a popular idea indeed (although not strictly a pop-up since they never pop-down!). Curtis supports its very own LFL at the train station in Brunswick.

- For libraries that want to take their services out of the library to potential library users elsewhere, a mobile pop-up is another good option. You can do this by simply packing up a stack of the most recent best sellers in a four-wheeled cart and taking it to the local senior housing.
- Or, you can get more creative. Pack up your books on a bicycle or wheelbarrow and take them to a farmer's market or local community event (during the summer in my town we have Music on the Mall on Wednesdays—a perfect opportunity). Are passersby going to stop at your pop-up and check out a million books? Probably not. However, you are putting your best assets and sales team (the library staff) out in a public location and giving them an audience in which discussions of books, reading, libraries, and the world can take place.

- Another idea for a pop-up would be a traveling library pop-up used not for the goal of circulating reading material but for marketing the library. The attraction of a pop-up is that it is unexpected and fun and that you, as the creator, are focused on creating a buzz. You could deck out several book carts with decorations and take it into local businesses or the police department or a local hospital and give away inexpensive, library-related products (bookmarks, mugs, balloons). Brunswick has a local car dealership that takes their mascot (a moose—not very surprising in this neck of the woods) into local businesses on Fridays to hand out donuts. Then they leave. That's the idea in a nutshell—and you wouldn't believe what an impact it can have! Don't underestimate the impact of *silly and fun* in creating a lot of community chatter.
- Pop-ups don't have to be about taking the library outside into the community. You can easily do a pop-up *in* the library. Consider that millennials as a generation are more about experiences than about things. Your library could offer a pop-up evening at the library with a local chef. People could purchase tickets, and the event would be about giving the chef and the library exposure and offering the participants an amazing experience.
- Another way you can incorporate a pop-up in your library space is to provide off-hours access for a special event. For some reason being in the library when it is closed is very appealing to both young and old. We raffled off the opportunity for a family to have a sleep-over in the library at a fundraising event, and a bidding frenzy broke out among several interested families!
- You could also consider making the library space available to local artisans or small businesses to do their own pop-up at the library. This would benefit local small businesses by providing a good audience for their products, the library would be supporting the community by providing a location with good traffic, and the library would benefit by having a fun destination event that would draw in potential users.

WILL THIS WORK AT MY LIBRARY?

If pop-ups are everywhere, are they still an idea that a library might want to explore? I think the answer is yes. Pop-ups are indeed everywhere, and the result is that people are getting more creative with their own versions of this phenomenon, which keeps them fresh and fun and something that people are constantly willing to try.

Be aware that pop-ups have to *look and seem* spontaneous and unplanned. However, the reality is that they take a lot of strategizing, developing, and hard work to pull off successfully. Make sure that everyone involved in your pop-up creation has good project management skills and the ability to deal well with last-minute issues.

If you want to hold a pop-up event in your library, it helps to have a space that is unique and that people would enjoy investigating. Curtis Library has two buildings: the original 1904 building, complete with a beautiful fireplace, high ceilings, and old maritime paintings; and the 1999 addition, which is modern, clean, and very functional in its appearance. The first building lends itself to pop-up events, such as the family sleep-over mentioned above.

However, if your library doesn't have a romantic, older space for pop-up events, get creative. Do you have a basement where the public isn't normally allowed that might lend itself to a Halloween pop-up? Do you have a rooftop that could be used? Even a parking lot can be turned into a usable space if you get imaginative.

Per the examples above, think carefully about your goals for a pop-up in order to ensure you are doing the right kind. Are you trying to create an opportunity for small businesses in your community? Promote the library? Provide a new service for library users? Defining your goal will go far in helping you decide what kind of pop-up will be most effective for your library to support.

AT THE END OF THE DAY

People love pop-ups because they are fun and different, and when you discover one, you feel like you know a secret. If a library pop-up happens somewhere in its community, it becomes a bit more special, surprising, and exciting—all attributes that will hopefully be ascribed to a library to help build a more modern personality for it.

> It is easy to live the expected and conventional. It's when you live the unexpected that you start having fun with your life.
> —RICHARD BACH

IF YOU WANT TO LEARN A BIT MORE

"15 Creative Examples of Branded Pop-Up Shops." Karla Cook. https://blog
.hubspot.com/marketing/creative-pop-up-events

"9 Brand Experiences That Popped Up and Into Our Hearts." Jonathan Ronzio.
Cramer. www.cramer.com/story/9-incredible-pop-ups-and-why-we-crave
-ephemeral-experiences/

"The Rise of Pop-up Events and What Event Planners Need to Know." Christina
Green. www.eventmanagerblog.com/the-rise-of-pop-up-events

"25 Eye Popping Pop-up Shop Examples to Inspire Your Small Business." Annie
Pilon. *Small Business Trends*. https://smallbiztrends.com/2017/10/pop-up
-shop-examples-small-business.html

"West Elm Local: Celebrating Community." West Elm. www.westelm.com/pages/
about-west-elm/our-commitments/local/

9

SILENT SPACES
WHAT WAS OLD IS NEW AGAIN

S ilence has become a valued commodity in today's world. We live with so much noise in our lives that when we find silence it seems precious and rare. As a library director I have heard over and over how important quiet is and how much people value it when they discover it still exists at the library.

Silence has become so rare that companies have started to identify quiet space as a need for employees in order to support creativity and mental health. To support this, they are developing meditation spaces and think tank spaces. Outdoor spaces are also being created for quiet and restoration.

The Lydia Group at Starrette Farm Retreat in North Carolina is a religious retreat center. They provide what they call silent day retreats on the second Friday of each month. There are no programs, but attendees are given access to the retreat center and its gardens for an opportunity to enjoy "a haven of silence where you can rest." Only twelve people can participate to ensure there is plenty of space and quiet.

Colleges are also participating in this process. Administrations have listened to their students' pleas for a place to go where the beeps and dings of technology can't be heard, where loud conversations on cellphones are not acceptable, where it's possible to just sit and think. In response colleges are creating relaxation rooms, meditation rooms, and quiet spaces. I have to admit that this baffled me somewhat, and I immediately thought, *Why don't students just go to the library if they want quiet?* Apparently, the library does not provide the white noise, yoga mats, or aromatherapy oils currently provided by relaxation rooms at some colleges. Ah, to be a student today!

Apparently, even at locations that are supposed to be loud, noisy, and fun, people get overwhelmed and then want a quiet space to relax and take a breath. In their blog *Mickey Visit*, there is an entire article about quiet places at Disneyland ("Relaxing at Disneyland"). Included are Tom Sawyer's Island, which includes walking trails and benches, the Grand Californian Hotel lobby, and the Redwood Creek Challenge Trail.

This direction in space use has extended to home spaces also. People who work from home are creating quiet rooms in which there are no electronic devices, clocks don't tick, and outside noise is eliminated as much as possible. These rooms are also being created for meditation spaces and for just plain quiet time. Interestingly, quiet in this context can also be compared to how we now define *uncluttered*. The idea being that if a space is visually cluttered, it is *noisy* and discourages creative thinking.

 IDEAS TO TRY

- It seems odd to provide ideas about quiet spaces to libraries because they have been known to be quiet for so many years. However, I think many libraries have been so focused on becoming community centers and on being open and engaging for all visitors that sometimes we lose sight of the value of quiet.

  Throughout my years as a library director I have often been told how much library users appreciate the value of quiet space in the library. Because Curtis Library is comprised of two connected buildings, it's easy to designate our original, historic building as the quiet space in the library. There are four rooms with high ceilings, deep carpets, and deep, leather furniture. We have discovered that library users, for the most part, police each other when it comes to quiet. If you can devise a quiet space like this in your library, I highly recommend doing so.

- If you aren't able to define an entire building as a quiet space, consider a quiet room that could be reserved by library users who desire such an area. If you don't have rooms that lend themselves to quiet study, consider designating tables in your library for quiet work.
- Another option is to lend noise-cancelling earphones to library users who desire quiet.
- You can also define certain spaces as silent at specific times each day or on specific days. So, you might have Silent Sundays or Student-Study Sundays in part of your library for the people in your community who desire quiet times or spaces.
- Because businesses are now interested in providing quiet for employees, many office furniture options meant to give people the space and structure needed to create a quite space are available. They generally have small walls on one side to discourage conversations. Some have a pod-like appearance. If space is at a premium, but you have sufficient funding to proceed, you might want to consider such furniture options to provide quiet.
- If all else fails (*Dare I say it?*), there is always the famous librarian's "shush!" to fall back on.

WILL THIS WORK AT YOUR LIBRARY?

I imagine this idea will work for every library, given our history. I think the only possible problem would be to create the appropriate balance between the quiet spaces and the busy ones. Libraries don't want to lose their hard-won reputation as community centers filled with energy and life by creating too much quiet space.

If you do have a good quiet place at your library, make sure to tell your community about it. Sometimes people may not feel comfortable opening a door or walking into a room when they are exploring your library. They may feel like they are intruding. This is one situation in which signs are useful, telling people that there is a quiet space within and that they should use it as such.

Also, don't forget to promote this as a library resource. I have had several small business entrepreneurs in my community tell me how useful a quiet space is for strategizing about their business and determining next steps. One owner told me that he marks out one day a month to come to the library and think. He finds that time incredibly valuable.

AT THE END OF THE DAY

Over the course of my career as a library director I have had any number of community members tell me how much they love what Curtis Library is doing and then follow up with the dreaded *but*. The *but* statement usually revolves around reminding me that there are a lot of people in my town who love a traditional library and want to make sure that isn't lost in the midst of all of the changes happening. So, I work hard to make sure there is always a place in the library for meditation, contemplation, writing, and the opportunity to sit and simply be quiet.

> Sometimes it's better to just be quiet, to not think of anything at all. Out of silence comes the greatest creativity.
> —JAMES ALTUCHER

IF YOU WANT TO LEARN A BIT MORE

"In a noisy world, some companies are cultivating silence in the workplace." Joyce Fownes. Hypepotamus. https://hypepotamus.com/community/workplace-quiet-spaces/

"Quiet space Fridays." The Lydia Group. www.thelydiagroup.com/quiet-space-fridays

"Relaxing Places at Disneyland: 9 Areas to Find Some Peace and Quiet." Lisa Stiglic. https://mickeyvisit.com/9-quiet-places-at-disneyland/

10

CO-WORKING SPACES
WITH A LITTLE HELP FROM MY FRIENDS

This is the age of the gig economy. Many people cobble together a living by having multiple jobs in multiple fields. Often those jobs don't include offices. This can be problematic when workers need the structure, interaction, or technology found when sharing office space with others. From this environment came the development of co-working spaces. Gig workers can rent space in an office for short chunks of time as needed. Office space can be rented with utilities and services shared with others, making it affordable for the noncorporate employee. Generally, a basic co-working space today provides space, technology support, and sometimes food and drink and networking opportunities. People using shared office spaces can come and go as they please, and frequently there is little or no interaction with others sharing the space.

Free-range workspaces are another variation on this concept. Instead of spaces that are broken up into small offices with shared copy rooms and breakrooms, free-range spaces are open, communal, and meant to facilitate interactions between people, including those who work in different industries.

In fact, the cross-pollination of ideas from different sectors is seen as a real benefit of using co-working space, since it encourages creativity and innovation.

Lifestyle co-working spaces are built around providing services for people who want a specific way of living and working. For example, some co-working spaces offer meditation, yoga, and vegetarian food. Others targeting young parents may offer day care and special programs for kids. Some may be dog-oriented, providing doggy day care, dog beds under desks, and water bowls situated as needed for pups.

There are also niche-specific co-working spaces. For example, Chisel is a co-working space specifically designed for attorneys in Washington, D.C. WorkChew turns Washington, D.C., restaurants into co-working spaces during off-hours. This gives gig workers a chance to get out of the house, and it gives the restaurants clientele during hours when they are not normally busy. The variations in co-working are increasing regularly, and it seems that most gig workers can find a type of space that works for them.

IDEAS TO TRY

Libraries are essentially the original co-working space. They have always provided space, technology, and support for independent workers. Public libraries are free; so, the price is right for young entrepreneurs, and reference librarians have always been a great resource when information is needed.

Today, libraries are finding they have more available space than they did twenty years ago. As more reading materials, especially in reference collections, go online, libraries are downsizing collections and taking out bulky furniture. By changing out bookshelves for tables and chairs, and by upgrading technology support, libraries are providing co-working spaces as an obvious new service. It brings people in the door and helps ensure that the local library continues to provide important and relevant community services.

- Create a space that will work for workers, but don't label it as such. Rather, make the space available to any and all who need a quiet place to work. Support services (food, special seating or lighting, reception services) will not be provided. Rather, this is a barebones approach. The library provides quiet and space and good Wi-Fi, and that's it.
- Your entire library is essentially a free-range co-working space. The library's resources (printing, copying, bathrooms, Wi-Fi) are all services provided to businesses. Meeting rooms can be reserved, and business

owners can use spaces for team meetings and brainstorming sessions. Quiet workspaces are available via the library's cubes. This is basically the model at Curtis Library today.

- If you have a space that can be "fenced off" as a co-working space, consider becoming a bit more generous with the support provided. You could provide a refrigerator with food/beverages or printers/copiers or meeting room space. Essentially, in this situation, you are creating a workspace within the library space.

- If your library is open in the evening, you could advertise it as a free co-working space for the night owls. Some libraries are experimenting with the idea of giving community members their own keys to the library so they can gain access after hours. Obviously, there is a lot you would need to work through to make that happen safely, but how is it really any different than giving people keys to a professional co-working space?

- You could even create your own niche co-working space by designating days of the week as co-working days at the library for specific industries. If you facilitated some simple networking at the beginning of the evening, it would be an efficient way of connecting people in the same industry.

WILL THIS WORK AT MY LIBRARY?

Some libraries have gone down this path by creating entire co-working environments within the library building. However, not all libraries have the space to create a stand-alone co-working environment. A library can still be a good option for co-working, as long as it has comfortable tables and chairs in a quiet part of the library, combined with high-speed Wi-Fi.

Another potential problem is that many towns already have co-working spaces that are commercial, meaning that they cost money to use. If this is true in your town, you will need to think about how to avoid becoming a source of competition for existing facilities, because that is guaranteed to create problems.

A third potential problem is the reaction of your library's users. Will they be happy to see the library bustling with business users, or will they view co-working spaces as a departure from the library's mission? You will need to think about how you market this concept to your traditional library users.

Finally, does your library have the staff to support an idea like this? If you follow a free-range model of co-working (simply promoting the library as a good place to work but not providing special services), you don't really need any more expertise from your librarians than they already offer. However, if you follow more of a concierge model, in which you provide services to coworkers, you may need to consider getting an administrative assistant to manage the work so that the librarians don't end up doing everything.

AT THE END OF THE DAY

Co-working spaces in libraries make total sense to me. People learn from each other, and community is built by the proximity of the learners. Isn't this what libraries have always been about?

> Tell me and I forget. Teach me and I remember.
> Involve me and I learn.
> —BENJAMIN FRANKLIN

IF YOU WANT TO LEARN A BIT MORE

"5 Co-working Spaces and Business Incubators in Libraries That Support Local
    Workers." Cat Johnson. Shareable. www.shareable.net/5-co-working-spaces
    -and-business-incubators-in-libraries-that-support-local-workers/
"Libraries as Co-working Spaces." Tech Soup for Libraries. http://techsoupfor
    libraries.org/blog/libraries-as-co-working-spaces

BESPOKE SPACES
I MADE THIS JUST FOR YOU

B espoke is not a word I knew well when I started doing research for this book. When I first ran across it, I thought it sounded like it came out of an Edwardian novel. I wasn't far off the mark.

Bespoke was a concept that came out of the British clothing industry. It referred to making a piece of clothing (shoes, jacket, pants, etc.) for one specific customer. Today, *bespoke* is being used constantly and has officially become trendy and a commonly used word in the hipster community.

In the August 8, 2016 *New York Times* article "Bespoke This. Bespoke That. Enough Already." by Jim Farber, the word and its meaning are explored:

> *The B word has become an increasingly common branding lure employed by interior design companies, publishers, surgeons and pornographers. There are bespoke wines, bespoke software, bespoke vacations, bespoke barber shops, bespoke insurance plans, bespoke yoga, bespoke tattoos, even bespoke medical implants.*

When applied to space, the concept of bespoke varies. In San Francisco there is a company by the name of Bespoke, which is, according to their website, ". . . a collection of tech-forward spaces, tailored for in-person inspiration." Essentially, the company develops co-working spaces tailored for gig workers in the tech industry. In this environment bespoke means created not for one individual but for people in one industry.

Bespoke is also a term heavily used in interior design to designate a specific aesthetic. For example, Bespoke Interior Design describes its aesthetic as "a study in balancing crisp, clean minimalism with the warmth of traditional architectural details." Bespoke spaces can also be spaces in which every element is created for one customer and nothing is mass-produced.

IDEAS TO TRY

Based on the popularity of the bespoke concept and knowing that today's consumers expect (based on their experience with the internet) to get what they want the way they want it, there is a power to this idea that is intriguing for libraries. The following are some of the ways the bespoke concept could be translated for use in a library:

- A common type of bespoke space is already offered by many libraries, though it is not meant for individuals but rather for groups that have a common, shared interest. An example of this is a library's genealogy or local history room. Generally, these rooms offer all of the resources that genealogists need, such as computers, databases, microfilm readers, genealogy books, and magazines. Groups appreciate a space dedicated to their areas of interest, and it certainly brings people into the library who may not come otherwise.
- Desks or carrels reserved for individuals are another example of bespoke spaces. When I was in college, at the beginning of senior year, you could reserve a carrel for yourself at the library for the entire senior year so that you had a consistent place to store your books and work on your senior thesis. Your desk became *your* space, complete with decorations, signs, and other things that personalized it. Many academic libraries still do this. Public libraries could designate a certain number of desks or spaces to be reserved each quarter by people who needed to write or study in a quiet place. The person could make the desk theirs, with the only caveat being that if they weren't using the space, it could be made available for public use.

- Smith College recently shared on Facebook opportunities for students at college libraries that I would categorize as bespoke concepts. The first is for students who don't want to carry books around campus. They can reserve a shelf at the library, which is labeled with their name, and they can then leave any books/materials on that shelf, to be used when they are in the library conducting research or studying. It is essentially the same idea as reserving a carrel but perhaps easier for a smaller library that doesn't have many carrels available for that purpose.
- The second bespoke idea created by Smith College is an app called Smithscape. The app itself doesn't create a bespoke space, but it allows a student to filter different available study spaces around the campus according to the type of space that works best for them based on their unique study process. If you want sunlight and some noise and activity, the app might direct you to the student center. If you like absolute silence, no interruptions, and little activity, it might recommend a lounge on the third floor of the science building. Brilliant, and the end result (a study space that is just the way that you want it to be) is absolutely bespoke!
- If your library isn't big enough to allow visitors to pick and choose the space that works best for them, you could instead provide tools that allow people to make their own bespoke space out of any location. For example, you could provide noise-cancelling headphones for people who need a greater degree of quiet than is normally available. For people who like to lounge more than sit, you could provide low-to-the-ground tables and chairs that allow folks to stretch out but still be seated. Or, you can provide a space with beanbags for adults!
- If your library has space outdoors around the library, you could create bespoke garden spaces along the lines of a community garden. People could reserve a garden space and create the type of garden they like. Libraries around the country have done this, resulting in spectacular flower gardens and vegetable gardens that provide produce all summer. The beauty of the idea is that it is bespoke in that each gardener is creating a totally unique space based on their interests and desires.

WILL THIS WORK AT MY LIBRARY?

How much is space at a premium in your library? If you find that certain areas of your library are rarely used by the public or staff, you may have an opportunity to create a bespoke space for a specific group of library users.

For example, at Curtis Library we had a large room originally designated for staff use, specifically technical services. Over time certain tasks that had originally been done in-house (such as covering books or cleaning CDs) started to become obsolete or were outsourced. This left a big, empty room available for other uses.

Genealogy was becoming a hot topic at that time, particularly among retired adults, who make up a large portion of Curtis's users. So, I turned the room into the Curtis Genealogy Room. It gave local genealogists a place to belong and genealogy volunteers a specific place in the library to *be* when they were helping other genealogists. Plus, it allowed us to put our genealogy collection of materials in one place, where they could be more easily accessed.

If public space is at a premium in your library, it can be harder to create a bespoke space for one specific group. You may have to use the same space for multiple groups, and that can make it much harder to make the space unique for one group.

This idea is also best if you can develop a bespoke space that can be easily changed if necessary. Over time the definition of *a place for me* tends to change. You need to not be so wedded to any specific idea that you can't let it go and move on to a new one. The Curtis Genealogy Room is heavily used on Fridays and weekends but doesn't have many visitors during the week. So, in view of high demand during the week for technology training space, we decided to use the Genealogy room for both purposes—technology during the week and genealogy on the weekend.

AT THE END OF THE DAY

There is great power in something that is made just for you. It appeals to most of us. In a confusing world, many people feel like they don't know where they belong or have lost the place they belong in. It is a powerful tool to enable people to feel like one place they always belong is at their space at the library.

> I had found my place in the world, the place I fit,
> the place I shined.
> —STEPHENIE MEYER

IF YOU WANT TO LEARN A BIT MORE

"A Bespoke Approach to Infinity Spa by Space Popular." *Habitus Living*.
    www.habitusliving.com/architecture/infinity-spa-space-popular
Bespoke: Tailored for tech. https://bespokesf.co
"Bespoke this. Bespoke that. Enough already." Jim Farbar. *The New York Times*.
    www.nytimes.com/2016/08/12/fashion/mens-style/bespoke-word-meaning
    -usage-language.html

12

MILLENNIAL-FRIENDLY SPACES
BLEISURE TRAVEL

Hotel lobbies aren't what they used to be. Ten or twenty years ago they were generally very grandiose, echoing spaces that you got through as quickly as possible on the way to your hotel room. Today, lobby spaces have become an extension of the hotel room, equipped with food, Wi-Fi, reading materials, and comfortable hangout spaces where hotel residents can sit and work, watch the world go by, eat dinner, read a book, or connect with other people.

This change is being driven to a large extent by millennials now old enough to start traveling for their jobs. Their generation does not want to stay in their hotel room any longer than necessary but are very comfortable hanging out in the lobby. Hotels have started to realize that their lobbies, rather than just being a neutral space, can actually become a selling point and help draw in younger hotel customers.

To make lobbies more enticing, hotels have created nooks where people can sit and work. There is food available (often for free or at minimal charge). The Wi-Fi is usually fast and free. Some hotels divide up the lobby into spaces more reminiscent of a house: a living room, library, playroom, and bar. Often there is local art on the walls to make the space cozier and more attractive.

Millennials are also blending their business and recreation trips (now officially called bleisure travel) because they don't have a great deal of extra income, and this type of travelling allows them to see places they wouldn't be able to afford if traveling on their own. These new hotel lobbies support what travelers need from a work trip (internet service, space for meetings) and while traveling for fun (comfort, play, relaxation).

An example of this can be seen in the Moxy Hotels, which were developed specifically by Marriott to target millennials. Their website (moxy-hotels .marriott.com) offers the following description of the Moxy Hotel (note in particular the phrase "Our lobbies are like living rooms with a bartender!"):

> *WE WANT YOU TO HAVE IT ALL*
>
> *You're new in town and you want to make a trip to remember. We totally get that. So, we've made sure the time you do spend at the Moxy is jam packed full of more fun than you thought you could have at a hotel. From yummy snacks and drinks, to games, to art, to secret hiding spots, to comfy couches to doze off in. Our lobbies are like living rooms with a bartender. Our guest rooms are like a cozy clubhouse you never want to leave, where you curl up in soft sheets, stream your favorite movie from our white-hot WiFi and cocoon for as long as you want. Because, #atthemoxy we want you to have it all.*

Another interesting example of this trend is Hotel EMC2 in Chicago. The hotel bills itself as " . . . at the Intersection of Art and Science." The décor in the hotel is anything but typical hotel blah. Portions of the property are decorated with art that is a reflection of the work done by mathematician Emmy Noether, a German scientist who focused on Einstein's theory of relativity in the 1930s. The hotel explains that it is dedicated to creativity, and it creates its "intimate environment" to encourage conversations and the exchange of ideas.

The goal of this somewhat unusual art is to spark the curiosity of hotel guests and engage them beyond the normal business travel transaction. This is exactly what millennials seem to find attractive—making travel an experience rather than just something that has to be endured. The EMC2 is part of the Autograph Collection Hotels by Marriott.

This concept is somewhat different from the Moxy in that it is obviously more inclusive in trying to attract other age groups. However, the same concepts being promoted by the Moxy are comfortable seating, an "intimate" environment, and a lobby broken up into different parts (living room, dining room, library) to make it seem more like a home. Plus, when you are finally ready to go back up to your room, there is a big desk to "fuel productivity."

IDEAS TO TRY

Productivity used to be seen as a surefire means of being promoted, and you were encouraged to sit at a desk and crank out your work. Today, people can find their productivity in whatever space works best for them. Some library patrons still want a traditional, quiet space where they can sit and work without interruption. However, many other patrons (particularly the younger ones) want comfortable spaces. Those can be hard to find in a traditional Carnegie, neoclassical, cold, austere, Greek temple that really hasn't changed in shape or design (unless it is brand new) in forty years.

If a millennial-friendly space (MFS) appeals to you and would be useful to your library's audience, the following ideas can help lead you down this road, even within the context of working with an austere, traditional space:

- Start with your technology. Your Wi-Fi must be fast and easily available. That is the first and most important criteria for creating an MFS in your library. Millennials (and pretty much everyone else in today's world) demand fast technology that works. Free but slow doesn't work anymore for libraries. Make sure your Wi-Fi is as fast as you can get it and that it works efficiently and effectively all the time. No one will tolerate slow Wi-Fi anymore.

> » While you are at it, make your Wi-Fi easily accessible. Don't require people to jump through hoops to use it. Get rid of sign-ins or the need to use a library card number. That puts a barrier in the way of the person trying to use this free service and can immediately put a crimp in the seamless interaction you are trying to create.

- Next, look carefully at your library building. Where can you create this space? It needs to be near your main entry doors, but you don't want it in the middle of traffic flow because that will reduce the comfort level for people using the space. You want to be near everything going on, so people can see and feel part of the energy, but you don't want to be smack in the middle of it.
- Consider your furniture. In the past twenty years many libraries decided they did *not* want people spending time in their library because it might bring in problematic behavior. As a result, library furniture is often hard and uncomfortable. I know this is the case at my library, which has a lot of beautiful teak outdoor benches that start to hurt your back the minute you sit down on them. Is there a way that you can provide some comfortable furniture in your MFS? You could do something as simple as working with the furniture you have by just adding cushions. Find a way to create comfort, even if it is only with a few pieces of furniture. Comfort is critical!
- Think seriously about your food and beverage policy. If you are still a library that doesn't allow either, this space might be a good way of trying out a new policy. Allow people to eat and drink there. It is amazing how much this makes a space immediately more accessible.
- Make sure your MFS is situated where people can talk in a normal tone of voice without disturbing other library users. You don't want to have to ask people to keep their voices down—there is no buzzkill like someone "shushing" you!
- Populate your MFS with things that might attract that specific group. For example, millennials are huge fans of board games. That age group is driving a renaissance of games like Monopoly and Clue, even as new games like Settlers of Catan are popularized. You could have gaming evenings in your lobby space and provide good food and drink to draw folks in.

- Don't forget to tell people about your MFS. This is a new idea for a library, and I can almost guarantee that millennials in your area will not be thinking about their local learning institution as *a place to be* unless you give them a nudge.

WILL THIS WORK AT MY LIBRARY?

This idea will work in almost any community because everyone appreciates comfort and an attractive space. I think it is a particularly good idea if you are trying to figure out how to attract millennials to your library. Such a space is designed with their perspective in mind, so hopefully it will resonate.

Don't try to create an MFS unless you enlist at least one millennial to help you in that process. This seems obvious, but in public libraries the staff are often middle-aged or older, and there may not be any millennials on the team. If there aren't any working at your library, go find at least one or two people in that age group who are willing to give you their perspective. Don't try such a project without exploring it first with people in the appropriate age group. Their expectations, interests, tastes, and perspectives are (of course) very different from those of baby boomers. If you want to create a space that will appeal to them, talk to them about it first.

Some of what you might do in an MFS might not appeal to some of your older library users. It is different from what they are used to, and they might complain. My response to this is "Yes, this is different. It is just like the teen space (which most library users are used to today). We are trying to bring young adults back into the library, and to do that, we need a space that appeals to them." I find this response works well because our older library users very much want younger folk to use the library, and it gives them an example of how we've already successfully created a targeted space.

AT THE END OF THE DAY

As I started researching and writing this chapter, I found myself feeling a bit cynical about the foibles of *the young folk*, meaning millennials. Who needs a hotel lobby (or a library) with big, soft sofas and places to hang out, and why should young adults be able to combine work travel with leisure travel? Isn't that kind of indulgent?

But then I stopped and thought about how this is exactly the attitude I don't want in my profession. I think we should be open to *all* ideas and be willing to challenge *all* of our perspectives to ensure the success of our libraries.

I also thought about how much nicer traveling would have been in my thirties if the experience had been more tailored to what I wanted at that age.

Finally, I thought that, really, as someone who wore elephant bellbottoms in the '60s and danced to the disco beat in the '70s, who am I to judge anyone about their preferences?

As a result of all this noodling, by the completion of this chapter, I was congratulating the millennials for having their own thing going on, and good for them!

> I'm not ashamed to be me. More than anyone else I know, I love my life and accept myself. What's wrong with being unique? I am proud of everything I am and will become.
> —JOHNNY WEIR

IF YOU WANT TO LEARN A BIT MORE

"8 trends sparking the hospitality sector." John Caulfield. *Building Design and Construction*. www.bdcnetwork.com/8-trends-sparking-hospitality-sector

Hotel EMC2. https://hotelemc2.com

Moxy Hotels. http://moxy-hotels.marriott.com/en

"The transformation of the hotel lobby." John Lally. *Today's Hotelier*. www.todayshotelier.com/2018/06/08/the-transformation-of-the-hotel-lobby-the-impacts-of-technology-and-young-traveler-trends/

13

SPACES SUPPORTING BIODIVERSITY
WHERE THE WILD THINGS ARE

G lobal warming and its impact on wildlife habitats has become a topic of interest across society. Architects in particular are beginning to think about how to create buildings with wildlife-friendly infrastructure incorporated into it, with the goal of replacing habitats that have been destroyed or are shrinking.

The architectural firm Terreform One has created a monarch butterfly habitat on the façade of a new, eight-story building (see photo on following page). The habitat will be a glass enclosure attached to the building structure and filled with vegetation specific to monarchs. Their food source will be amplified by a rooftop garden with butterfly-focused plants, as well 3-D concrete that will give the butterflies a place to land. The structure looks very futuristic, but its purpose is simple and straightforward—to support the life stages of the monarch butterfly.

Another example of the bio-supportive architectural concept is the inclusion of rooftop beehives in buildings in Norway. The hives were created with the goal of calling attention to how important bees are in plant pollination

and growth. Their Vulcan Beehives are made of wood, incorporate beehive imagery, and were created by the design/architecture firm Snohetta.

The Boulder Public Library in Boulder, Colorado, has already "beecome" (See what I did there?) a home for honeybees. The library has two hives on its roof, tended by a local bee advocacy group, the BeeChicas. The library offers programming focused on the bees, and extra honey from the hives is used in the library's café. Other libraries that have adopted this idea show the bees 24/7 on live video feeds. The public finds it mesmerizing, and it provides a great opportunity to educate viewers on the critical importance of bees in our ecosystem.

Another example of wildlife-oriented space development is the creation of wildlife corridors made up of underpasses and overpasses by roads. The goal is to create a safe *highway* for animals, insects, toads, turtles, and other creatures so they can avoid roads that otherwise might kill them.

Bat habitats have become a component of space creation, particularly as the bat populations across the United States have suffered from white-nose syndrome. Some communities, such as Austin, Texas, have embraced their bats and made them part of the local community. At the end of each day, it has become commonplace for community residents to watch literally millions of bats streaming out from local bridges to go hunting.

Birds are often the focus of creating this type of space design. Green rooftop gardens benefit them by providing both food and places to nest. Some buildings are now being built with bricks that jut out from the *skin* of the building's façade to provide nesting sites for swallows and thrushes. Osprey will happily take up residence on tall buildings, and similar nesting platforms are being provided for them at various locations.

Volvo has created a fascinating seawall in Australia that is hexagonal in shape and replicates the root system of mangroves in the design on its façade, with the goal of promoting biodiversity (the mangrove design attracts small sea creatures that attach themselves there and thrive). Because the wall is made from recycled plastics, it also contributes to the sustainability of the environment.

Green roofs are another method by which buildings can support wildlife habitat development. When wildflowers are grown across an entire roof, it helps reduce "ecological habitat fragmentation." Green roof creation can substantially mitigate the destruction caused by urban development.

IDEAS TO TRY

The beauty of spaces that support biodiversity is that they can be developed into big ideas (a seawall in Sydney Harbor) and small (beehives, bat houses). The following are some ways that libraries are already experimenting with this idea:

- Create a butterfly garden at your library (see photo on following page). You don't need much space to plant milkweed, black-eyed Susans, phlox, or butterfly bushes, and they all grow happily in almost any space. If you don't have space for an entire garden, or your environment is too hot/dry/cold, consider planting container gardens or rooftop gardens that can be maintained more easily.

- If you have the wrong environment for a butterfly garden, consider creating a rooftop garden that will work with your outdoor conditions. Of course, every building has different codes and rules that have to be incorporated into planning, but even small gardens could help local wildlife like birds find nesting spaces and provide flowers for pollinators. If possible, you could open up the space to library users, but that isn't core to this idea—it is just a nice add-on!
- Ask local beekeepers to help create a beehive habitat on the roof of your library. Bees are critical for pollination and having such a visible symbol of support on the library makes a great statement about the need to support wildlife.
- If you have bats locally, build bat habitats and place them on your library roof. I can envision a *bat house build-out*, much like a build-out for Little Free Libraries.

WILL THIS WORK AT MY LIBRARY?

These ideas are all reasonably simple and can be implemented without dealing with major hurdles.

So, why is this idea useful to libraries? Every project you do that creates support for local wildlife can also be a wonderful way of obtaining positive PR for your library. They can also beautify your library and make it more relevant to the part of your community that is interested in habitat sustainability. On top of all that, these projects are fun for everyone to do.

Do keep in mind that as more habitats are being created across cities and towns, they often do not work toward a common goal. It does make sense before embarking on any of these ideas to research what is being done already to support wildlife in your community so that your library might build on what already exists rather than starting something new that might or might not be useful.

AT THE END OF THE DAY

The more urban our lives are, the more we miss the presence of nature. Using library spaces as a way to bring nature more intimately into our lives, and as a tool to educate about the importance of maintaining biodiversity, fits directly into the traditional role of libraries to educate and inform and can only help make both our libraries and our communities better.

> Cherish the natural world because you're part of it
> and you depend on it.
> —SIR DAVID ATTENBOROUGH

IF YOU WANT TO LEARN A BIT MORE

"File Under Bee: Libraries open up to beekeeping." Rachel Chance. *American Libraries Magazine.* https://americanlibrariesmagazine.org/2019/09/03/file-under-bee-library-beekeeping/

"Green Infrastructure: Wildlife Habitat and Corridors." The American Society of Landscape Architects. www.asla.org/ContentDetail.aspx?id=43534

"Wildlife Habitat-Incorporating Buildings." Kalina Nedelcheva. *Trend Hunter.* www.trendhunter.com/trends/butterfly-habitat

"Wooden Rooftop Beehives." Jamie Danielle Munro. *Trend Hunter.* www.trend hunter.com/trends/vulkan-beehive

14

PLACEMAKING
YOUR COMMUNITY

When I was in college, I majored in art history with a particular focus on architecture. I was fascinated by the ways different architects, such as Frank Lloyd Wright and Charles Moore, created architecture that was uniquely rooted in its location. Falling Water by Wright is considered to be one of the best examples of a building that works with its environment versus trying to dominate its space. It is human-scaled, blends into the natural environment (complete with a stream flowing through the bottom of the house), and is unique.

Today, there is an entire movement called *placemaking*, which is a component of urban design. Its goal is to create environments within a community that are unique to that community, its geography, its assets, and the people who live there. Placemaking tries to create something of value for a community in underutilized spaces, to create "more there there" (misusing Gertrude Stein's quote) using the input of the people who live in that space to ensure ideas that are viable and seen as having value.

However, placemaking is more than urban design or architectural planning. It is about amplifying what is unique, special, and wonderful about a location to create a place where people don't just pass through but want to spend time. And, when people congregate, energy is created and dead zones (under-utilized, under-appreciated spaces) disappear.

All of the ideas in this book are, at their heart, about how to do placemaking in the microcosm of a library, both inside and outside. They are meant to create a library that is unique, wonderful, inviting, and designed around what its users want. I've focused on space ideas that can be adapted by libraries, but there are many other creative and intriguing ideas that might also benefit libraries.

IDEAS TO TRY

Here are some additional placemaking ideas that showcase the power of thinking creatively in every square inch of your library. Good luck, have fun, and check out the Project for Public Spaces (PPS) website (www.pps.org), which focuses on the concept of placemaking.

- **Lighter, quicker, cheaper.** In "A New Guide to Balancing Mobility and Humanity on Main Street," PBS explores "the lighter, quicker, cheaper transformation of public spaces." One example of this idea is the creation of seasonal, one-time events to call attention to the potential value or importance of a space or an organization, or to inspire community conversations about ideas that will have an impact on everyone, such as renovating a building, building a park, or creating bicycle-friendly streets.
  - » Curtis Library does a once-a-year "How-to Festival" that started inside the library but has now expanded to the street outside the library. It was not planned as a "lighter, quick, cheaper transformation of a public space," but it has become that. On a Saturday morning in the fall for four hours, the library provides classes, speakers, educators, and exhibits on topics of every size and shape, from beekeeping, to tiny houses, to rug hooking, to making your own lip balm. The goal of the festival is to get people to experience the library, have the opportunity to learn and enjoy themselves, and celebrate the wonderful community in which we live. The staff members who create the program have grown more creative not only about using the library's space but also incorporating the

space outside the library and across the street in the sanctuary of our neighboring Unitarian church. We invite our neighbors to the event and include the grocery store at the end of the street, so the event also becomes very much about community-building.

» The How-to Festival is not unique. Any library could experiment with their version of it. What is wonderful about it is that it makes the square block around the library attractive, fun, and intriguing enough for people to want to explore it, even if they don't normally go to library events. The festival is easily accessible, and everything is free to attend, so there is no financial commitment. Plus, it is intergenerational, so people of all ages can find something interesting. It has proved to be a very powerful tool for Curtis Library in our efforts to build awareness, connections, and an ongoing dialog with our community members.

- **Creative placemaking.** A variation of placemaking is *creative placemaking*, in which community members, artists, and other stakeholders use arts and culture as a way to implement change or call attention to a location in the community.

  » An example of this would be a group of citizens working to create public art installations in a community as a way of increasing the viability of public spaces that would normally not be noticed by most people and might even become hazardous spots because of the lack of foot traffic. Some examples might include empty lots, train or bus stations, alleyways, or drive-through streets. Creative placemaking can help turn all of these locations from spaces of no value into places with personality and vitality, where people want to spend time.

  » Creative placemaking can be challenging. You are putting art into a public space (and more often than not, a space that has not had a lot of people using it) and trusting that it will not be abused. You are also making assumptions about the type of art that people will be interested in seeing. This process takes a certain willingness to plug your nose, jump into the water, and hope for the best!

  » At Curtis we embarked on creative placemaking because a library donor who was moving offered to donate two outdoor statues to the library, since he would no longer have a place for them at his new home. After seeing the sculptures, I couldn't say no because they were both lovely. We decided to experiment. We had a small

wall by the public sidewalk that frequently was used as a place where local folks would sit and occasionally create issues. We decided that rather than trying to keep people off the wall, we were going to turn that area into a garden with one of our new sculptures featured in it.

Our hope was that by making the space attractive and inviting, it would create a positive energy that would reduce or eliminate the problems that tended to occur there. The idea worked, but it took some time and perseverance. Within a month of putting the statue in the new garden, it was tipped over. We put it back up and did a better job of anchoring it so it couldn't be pushed over as easily. Someone then decorated the statue with egg salad! We cleaned it up. Then . . . the problems stopped! Ten years later the statue continues to sit in its garden, and people no longer hang out there and create problems. Kids now run around the lawn by the statue, and people frequently stop to admire it. Curtis Library has a new place.

» In the past libraries would often try to avoid behavioral issues by eliminating or closing off the locations where problems occurred (empty hallways, nooks in the library, etc.). However, placemaking takes a different approach in that it embraces *orphan* spaces and turns them into attractive, interesting places where people see value in spending time. When you have more people in a space,

fewer problems occur. I love the positivity of this approach, and with some patience and perseverance it does seem to work.

- **Parklets or street seats.** An example of placemaking that I find particularly appealing and viable for libraries is the creation of *parklets*, or street seats. Parklets are just what they sound like. A parking space is transformed into a tiny park by putting flowers/trees/shrubs in the parking space, along with seating of some sort to encourage people to stop, sit, and chat. Parklets are sometimes created by community groups or an association of local retailers, or sometimes just by local citizens.

  » A more complicated parklet occurs when the sidewalk is purposely *bumped out* so that the sidewalk extends into what would otherwise be a parking space. Stores use them to put out seating or displays, and restaurants use them for outside seating. However, the end result is the same—a place that encourages human beings to stop and linger and enjoy the space.

  » Parklets are an enticing idea because most libraries have parking spaces for the public, thereby immediately providing the most important element of the idea. I also appreciate that you can make a parklet as simple or ornate as you want (within community guidelines). You can also create a pop-up parklet for special events or programs. If you don't have a lot of parking, you might consider creating a parklet next to your parking area instead of in it.

» Curtis Library has a lot of brick sidewalk at the main entrance of the library. In the summer it was always hot, dry, dusty, and not at all appealing. A group of Curtis librarian gardeners decided to improve the space around the parking area and make the front entrance to the library more friendly and attractive by creating barrel planters and simple café chairs and tables that could be moved in and out of the library every night. The barrel planters and chairs/tables improved the space so much and so quickly that it was a bit of a surprise. Today, what was originally an empty space that had only attracted problems has become a comfortable, enticing community outdoor space where people chat, kids get tutored, and people sit and watch the world go by. That's the real draw of a parklet—it creates all sorts of wonderful interactions.

- **Carnegie libraries as placemakers.** Is some part of your library a historic building? So many libraries were created as Carnegie institutions in the early 1900s or were created as a response to the Carnegie push for public libraries in the United States that, at least in New England, it was very common to find a Carnegie building attached to a newer library addition. If your library is a Carnegie building or a historic building, you have the components of a wonderful placemaker.

» Carnegie libraries are beautiful and unique. Consider how you can keep the uniqueness of that building, even as your need for space in your library evolves. Space is at a premium at Curtis Library, as is money for building work. However, I have made a commitment to restore elements of the library's older building (built in 1904), rather than replace them with more modern building elements (which are often much less expensive than a restored item would be).

» Restoration helps ensure that the original library will stay in its historic form, which is beautiful and much valued by the community. So, even though it would be much easier and less expensive to replace rather than restore the original library's doors, we have gone with restoration to ensure we keep the *voice* of the library unchanged.

» The same approach is used on the exterior of the original building. Slowly over time we have created small gardens on either side of the 1904 building's entrance. The plants are what might have been used in 1904. Large planters were also added to either side of the entrance, and they were chosen specifically because they fit into the historical time period of the building. The plantings have done a beautiful job of enhancing the building's exterior, and more and more often we are finding people sitting on the steps of the building, enjoying the space.

- **Create a seat.** One great way of placemaking both inside and outside your library may be the simplest thing ever: provide comfortable seats where more than one person can sit at a time. Benches work. Small groups of chairs work. Then, put up a sign and say something like "chatting with your neighbor encouraged here."
  - » Chat benches were created by a town in England in an effort to combat loneliness in the community, and they have been a big success. One staff member at Curtis saw an article about the benches in *The Washington Post* and immediately asked if we could do something similar at the library. I loved the idea and said yes. We will soon have our very own chat bench at the library.
- **Document the street where your library lives.** I think this idea, which originated in an article on curbed.com, makes for a perfect placemaking project for libraries. The idea is simply to document the street or block where you live, or in this case, where your library is located. Get your community involved and ask for their help in taking pictures or sharing stories of the lives of those who live/work/play on the block. The idea is that by being aware of the street/block as a *place* that is worthy of being documented, you are helping create that space and building awareness that it exists as a unique entity.
  - » Have a location in your library where your documentation lives. Take pictures in different seasons. Document how the street life changes if you add a parklet or upgrade gardens or add a chat bench. Ask children to get involved by drawing pictures of what they see. Share this information with the larger community.
  - » Photographs are rapidly becoming the most shared form of communication in our society. Use them to tell the story of your library community, and in that process, help create more *place*.
- **The power of light.** Light is a powerful, inexpensive, and relatively easy way to create place. I learned this lesson from several of the staff at Curtis. Every time we had a special event, they would add twinkle lights or table lights or luminaria as part of the event. Those lights did so much to turn library events into something special. Now, we regularly use lighting as part of our special events, and those lights help a great deal to create ambiance and a sense that people are entering a distinctive place when they walk into the event.

» You can also use the same idea outside the library to help amplify its role as an important place in the community. Light can come in many forms. The Lucius Beebe Memorial Library in Wakefield, Massachusetts, hosts an annual Carved Jack-o'-Lantern display on the front steps of the library around Halloween. Several hundred pumpkins are carved by local art students and lit on one night, creating a display that hundreds of people turn out to see. The library becomes *the* place to be on that night!

» Or, borrow an idea from the Coastal Maine Botanical Gardens in Boothbay, Maine. Every year they wrap the gardens in twinkle lights, creating "Gardens Aglow" in December. What used to be a very quiet season with few visitors has become as busy as their summer season, with thousands of people buying tickets to see the display at nighttime. A library could certainly pick a time of the year and wrap itself in lights as a way of celebrating and creating a *special place* in the community.

» Another way that a library can use lighting is to turn the library building into a giant screen and project onto it. I first saw this done at the Bunker Hill Monument in Boston. The monument (which is a smaller version of the Washington Monument) became a screen onto which images were projected, telling a story about families and crime in the Charlestown neighborhood. It was very powerful because it brought hundreds of people into that neighborhood who had probably never been there before and gave them a way to relate to the environment. A library could do this quite simply using today's technology. The building could become a canvas for videos produced by local teenagers or oral histories given by library users, or it could project the neighborhood documentation written about earlier in this chapter. The possibilities are endless.

- **The longest table.** Community and placemaking come together nicely in the "longest table" movement. Community members are invited to attend a dinner at one extremely long table, with the goal of meeting people from their community and to exchange ideas about specific topics. A free meal is provided for all, and attendees must be willing to sit with people they don't know. In some communities the longest table has ended up seating hundreds of attendees.

» Some communities use an event like this as a fundraiser, which I'm sure is interesting. However, I think it has the most value when the meal is provided for free, and the focus is on meeting your neighbors and providing input about specific community questions or issues. It certainly is placemaking, especially if held outside. Imagine a table for three hundred people and how that could draw attention both to your library and the issue at hand.

AT THE END OF THE DAY

Over my library career I have come to the conclusion that one of the most important things that a library does is to make the concept of community real and concrete. A library embodies the values of the people who use and support it. It tells the world "this is who we are and what matters to us." Libraries create a powerful, vibrant place that helps define the personality of its community in a vivid way. With libraries our shared, communal life is so much more interesting and compelling than it would be without.

> It is good people who make good places.
> —ANNA SEWELL, *BLACK BEAUTY*

IF YOU WANT TO LEARN A BIT MORE

"Creative Placemaking." National Endowment for the Arts (NEA). www.arts.gov/ artistic-fields/creative-placemaking

"4 Examples of Powerful Placemaking." Kaid Benfield. CityLab. www.citylab.com/ design/2013/01/3-examples-powerful-placemaking/4329/

"Four types of placemaking." Robert Steuteville. Congress for the New Urbanism (CNU). www.cnu.org/publicsquare/four-types-placemaking

"101 Small ways you can improve your city." Patrick Sisson and Alissa Walker. *Curbed*. www.curbed.com/2016/9/22/13019420/urban-design-community -building-placemaking

"This town's solution to loneliness? The 'chat bench.'" Cathy Free. *The Washington Post*. www.washingtonpost.com/lifestyle/2019/07/17/this-towns-solution -loneliness-chat-bench/

"What Is Placemaking?" Project for Public Spaces. www.pps.org/article/what-is -placemaking

PHOTO CREDITS

Photo on page 2   "Ford Foundation" by Timothy Vollmer, Flickr, licensed under CC BY 2.0 (https://creativecommons.org/licenses/by/2.0/), https://www.flickr.com/photos/sixteenmilesof string/19375212824

Photo on page 3   "Skywalk Glass Bridge," Adobe Stock Photo 140114044

Photo on page 5   "Tree in children's area at Curtis Memorial Library" by Jamie Doucett

Photo on page 7   "Vertical Succulent Wall" by Chris Hunkeler, Flickr, licensed under CC BY-SA 2.0 (https://creativecommons.org/licenses/by-sa/2.0/), https://www.flickr.com/photos/chrishunkeler/8850172234

Photo on page 7   "Little Water Girl" by Abraham Schechter

Photo on page 12   "Umbrellas" by Curtis Memorial Library

Photo on page 13   "Owls in the mezzanine" by Curtis Memorial Library

Photo on page 14   "Lobster buoys" by Curtis Memorial Library

Photo on page 16   "Sunflower reading nook" by Jamie Doucett

Photo on page 17   "Bicycle wheels" by Curtis Memorial Library

Photo on page 33   "Curtis Memorial Library mezzanine" by Jamie Doucett

Photo on page 35   "Volunteer station" by Curtis Memorial Library

Photo on page 40   "Google Bikes" by Travis Wise, Flickr, licensed under CC BY 2.0. (https://creativecommons.org/licenses/by/2.0/), https://www.flickr.com/photos/photographingtravis/33241265870

Photo on page 42   "Curtis Memorial Library banners" by Jamie Doucett

Photo on page 43   "Curtis Memorial Library bookmarks" by Jamie Doucett

Photo on page 53   "Curtis Memorial Library Little Free Library" by Curtis Memorial Library

Photo on page 63   "Young casually dressed employees at work in coworking office," Adobe Stock photo 175714144

Photo on page 74   "Moxy Hotel in New Orleans" by Kristina D.C. Hoeppner, Flickr, licensed under CC BY-SA 2.0 (https://creativecommons.org/licenses/by-sa/2.0/), https://www.flickr.com/photos/4nitsirk/38542127924